RAPTURE FICTION

AND THE EVANGELICAL CRISIS

CRAWFORD
GRIBBEN

SERIES EDITORS
DR JOHN D. CURRID AND ROBERT STRIVENS

 EVANGELICAL PRESS

 EVANGELICAL PRESS

Evangelical Press
Faverdale North Industrial Estate, Darlington, DL3 0PH England
email: sales@evangelicalpress.org

Evangelical Press USA
PO Box 825, Webster, NY 14580 USA
email: usa.sales@evangelicalpress.org

www.evangelicalpress.org

First published 2006

 The EMMAUS series has been created to speak directly to pastors, teachers and students of the Word of God on those issues that impact on their everyday ministry and life.

British Library Cataloguing in Publication Data available

ISBN-13 978 0 85234 610 5   ISBN 0 85234 610 7

Contents

For Daniel

PREFACE

JESUS CHRIST WILL SOON RETURN TO THE EARTH. This book, like the *Left Behind* series and the other rapture novels it discusses, finds its hope in that statement's truth. Nothing that this book argues should therefore be understood as in any way underplaying the significance of our Lord's second coming, or its central importance in consistent Christian living. The New Testament documents shine with the anticipation of glory, and this book must not dull that hope.

Rapture Fiction and the Evangelical Crisis attempts to retain rapture novels' enthusiasm for the return of Jesus Christ at the same time as it examines their presentation of the gospel. Its most basic argument is that rapture novels have emerged from an evangelicalism that shows signs of serious theological decay. In their descriptions of conversion and Christian living, the *Left Behind* series, with many of its antecedents and imitators, demonstrates a sometimes inadequate understanding of the gospel, the church and the Christian life. These novels are some of the best-selling 'evangelical' titles in the world, but the faith they represent cannot be identified with the historic orthodoxy of evangelical Protestantism, the 'faith which was once delivered unto the saints' (Jude 3). The novels' combination of theological inadequacy and massive popularity is evidence that evangelicalism is now in serious crisis.[1]

Perhaps many readers will pick up this book expecting an analysis or even a refutation of the prophetic scheme the novels advance. This book does not provide any such analysis. 'Dispensationalism' (the term, describing the novels' prophetic expectation, is explained in chapter one) has never lacked its critics, and the section on further reading suggests a number of titles that offer helpful discussions of its eschatology. Instead, this book concentrates on the most important of the novels' ideas. The dispensational account of redemptive history and eschatology does deserve serious consideration, but its importance is overshadowed by concern about the most basic elements of Christian truth. This book concentrates on the novels' theology of conversion, the church and the Christian life, and argues that their presentation of these ideas regularly represents something fundamentally different from Biblical Christianity.

There are several reasons why this book does not attack dispensationalism. Firstly, it is essential to remember that differences about the end of the world are insignificant when compared to differences about the gospel. It is also important to remember that a renewed commitment to the gospel does not demand that dispensationalism be left behind. The history of evangelicalism includes many individuals who have combined their dispensationalism with a whole-hearted commitment to the central ideas of the classical evangelical faith. John MacArthur and

James Montgomery Boice, for example, have each been powerful spokesmen for dispensationalism at the same time as they have powerfully defended the gospel of grace.[2] In addition, the writer of this book was converted and baptised among dispensationalists, and owes an immense debt to the early training he received. The individuals I most admired in the 'Brethren' assemblies of my youth were individuals whose commitment to dispensationalism did not engender anything like the crisis that fuels the narratives of *Left Behind*. For these and other reasons, this book has not been written to dispute dispensational pre-millennialism; it is for readers to draw their own conclusions about its broader validity. Instead, this book has been written to encourage a reconsideration of a series of novels that are increasingly identifying their own peculiar version of dispensationalism with the heart of the historic evangelical faith.

The idea for this book has been developing since I began to read and watch rapture fiction in my early teens. I would like to thank everyone who has encouraged me to consider the message of Bible prophecy along the way – especially those who have (all too frequently) proved my opinions wrong! Among the latter, particular thanks are due to Revd Professor David McKay, of Reformed Theological College, Belfast, whose lectures on dispensationalism have been a continuing resource; Simon Wheeler, of Ramsgate, Kent, and Mark Sweetnam, of Trinity College, Dublin, have also been sharp-sighted and sagacious critics of my ideas. My understanding of Brethren history has been greatly assisted by conversations with Dr Timothy Stunt, and through my involvement with the Brethren Archivists and Historians Network. Chapter two is heavily dependant on Dr Stunt's research, as detailed in the footnotes. David, Simon and Mark each commented on an early draft of this book, though I take full responsibility for any errors that may remain. I would like to thank Oxford University Press for their permission to re-use material that originally appeared in *Literature and Theology* 18:1 (2004). I would also like to thank Angus and Jenny Macleod, of Ayr, for their long-standing encouragement and support; and, in Northern Ireland, Revd Jack Lamb, John Grier and Revd David Sutherland, for the stimulus they provided for this project. I also thank Barry Horner for his comments on the manuscript and Randall Pederson and David Clark at Evangelical Press for their invaluable assistance in its production.

Deepest thanks are due to my mum and dad and to Pauline, who have variously read the books, watched the films, hid from the guillotines, and encouraged the hope. 'Even so, come, Lord Jesus.'

Crawford Gribben
April 2006

Chapter 1

THE RAPTURE FICTION PHENOMENON

'I'd say if you're going to write fiction, you ought to get a novel deal and go for it.'[1]

FORGET ABOUT HARRY POTTER. The most successful series of novels in the world today do not describe the adventures of a trainee wizard, but events that many evangelicals associate with the end of the age. *Left Behind*, an expanding series of fourteen novels written by two overtly evangelical authors, is the most astonishing English-language literary phenomenon of the early twenty-first century. Since 1995, when the first of the novels was published, the series has sold over sixty million titles. *Desecration* (2001), the ninth book in the series, became the world's top selling work of adult hardback fiction in the year of its release. The authors of the series, Jerry B. Jenkins and Tim LaHaye, have claimed never to have expected this level of popularity, but they have not been slow in exploiting it to the full. The series' spin-offs have included a board game, a spectacular website, clothes, music CDs, comic books, and a dramatisation of (so far) three titles, the first of which was the most expensive Christian film ever made.[2] Put the sales in perspective: these novels have sold over half as many copies in ten years as J. R. R. Tolkien's *The Lord of the Rings* has in fifty.[3] Whatever you think of it, *Left Behind* is a publishing sensation.

FASCINATION WITH THE END OF THE WORLD

With this remarkable degree of popularity, it would be hard to imagine that *Left Behind* simply emerged from nowhere. Recent years have seen a spectacular revival of interest in apocalyptic themes. In the late 1990s, a number of films were released with a strong 'end of days' focus. One film even had that title: in *End of Days* (1999), Arnold Schwarzenegger played the policeman whose job it was to prevent the devil bringing an end to history by finding his bride in New York. *Deep Impact* (1998) imagined that life on earth could be destroyed in a collision with a comet. While disaster films have always been popular, their prominence at the end of the 1990s suggested that cinema directors were catering for a particularly anxious film-going public.

This recent 'boom in doom' is part of a much larger fascination with the end of the world. The late twentieth-century interest in the apocalypse was regularly grounded in the realisation that the end of the world could be more imminent than had been expected. The series of conflicts during the second half of the twentieth century proved that global apocalypse was no longer a divine monopoly. Humanity itself now possessed the power to wreak the destruction of the planet, and the atomic end to World War Two, together with the nuclear stand-off of the Cold War and the genocide created by the implosion of African and European states, suggested that the world's so-called civilised powers might not always be reluctant to resort to ultimate weaponry and solutions of mass death. In the aftermath of the Cold War, concerns about the melting of the polar ice caps and the rapid spread of nuclear power among 'failed' and 'rogue' states encouraged political commentators to use apocalyptic language more regularly, and perhaps with greater justification, than ever before.

Despite the apparent novelty of these modern dangers, however, this kind of fascination with the end of the world is nothing new. Apocalypticism (the expectation of a cataclysmic end to history) and millennialism (the hope for a better world before the end of history) have both had many exponents.[4] Both themes can be found in the Bible, throughout the culture of the ancient near east, and in a variety of other civilisations.[5] In recent centuries, Islamic fundamentalists have been driven by an overtly apocalyptic hope as they worked towards a world controlled by the laws of their faith. Throughout the last 150 years, Marxism has been an inherently millennial political creed, working towards a utopian world in which workers will control the means of production. Perhaps the most obvious example of twentieth-century millennial thinking is found in the ideology of the Nazis, whose language of a 'thousand-year *reich*' was clearly modelled on the thousand-year reign of Christ described in Revelation 20.[6] Whether they have imagined the imminent end of all things, or the imminent (and potentially violent) improvement of the world, thinkers from many backgrounds have concentrated on the transforming possibilities of the end of the age.

Y2K and 9-11

But living at the end of the age can generate as much fear as hope. Perhaps it was the former, rather than the latter, that dominated in the surge of apocalyptic and millennial concern at the end of the 1990s.

For many people, of course, discussion of 'the millennium' has been intrinsically associated with the turn of the year 2000. 'Y2K' was certainly the excuse for a great deal of fireworks – who could forget the breathtaking displays beamed from Australia as that nation celebrated the new year, new century and new millennium hours before the rest of the West? But many of those who sat in their homes watching festivities on the other side of the world must also have been keeping an anxious eye on the electricity. For many, the hours before the clock struck twelve were as likely to bring devastation as delight. Throughout the late 1990s, a variety of public figures had grown intensely concerned by fears that the year 2000 would herald a technological crash, as computers across the world failed to come to terms with the dating of the new century. Fears were raised that government computers, for example, would fail to provide for welfare support, and that the sudden plunge into economic chaos would result in large-scale rioting and looting across the West. Some of those who took these claims seriously – and their number included many significant figures in business and technology – suggested that prudent savers should withdraw their investments, buy gold, and, variously, guns and generators, to sit out the chaos with the comfort of a well-stocked fridge.[7] The problem, as many other prudent investors realised, was that the widespread adoption of this strategy would cause the very economic uncertainty it feared, by generating a run on the banks that would plunge the West into an inflationary nightmare.

Others in the run-up to the year 2000 were concerned by the political repercussions of religious fears. The mass suicides of several UFO cults in the later 1990s indicated that others outside the Christian mainstream were adapting elements of Christian millennialism in distinctly non-traditional ways. Perhaps more surprising was the concentration on the year 2000 in the literature of radical Islamists. Across the near east, and in Britain more often than in North America, Islamic radicals pointed to the year 2000 as part of a larger time scale that, they believed, would include the final destruction of the United States. The emphasis on the year 2000 was perhaps unexpected, given the fact that the Muslim calendar began in the year 622. But the publications of some of these radical writers were demonstrating that Muslims were turning to the Bible, as well as the Qur'an, to discover the details of the end. 'The Hour' – the end of all things in Islamic theology – was being documented using information derived from Daniel and Revelation, as well as a number of evangelical publications.[8] Some of the literature was imagining that the end times had begun with the Arab-Israeli conflict, and that the near future would herald the rise of the *Dajjal*, a demonic Jew who would use a global conspiracy to gain control over all but the most faithful Islamic states. His reign was expected to end only with the return of Jesus, whose coming was to bring judgement and the end of the world. These apocalyptic hopes generated a disturbing political momentum. 1987 was both the beginning of the *Intifada* and the anticipated fulfillment of an 80-year-old prophecy of global apocalypse.[9] In the late 1990s, radical Islamists portrayed the USA as the great Babylon described in Revelation 17, and some argued that the 'antichrist' figure was Saddam Hussein, who was, they believed, operating under the covert guidance of Israel. The year 2000 was believed to be a key to his ultimate fall.[10]

But this combination of apocalyptic fear and political assumption was not at all limited to the literature of radical Islam. A number of Christian approaches to the end of the world had an equally political edge. In Russia, Orthodox clerics debated whether changes to the tax system suggested the imminent arrival of the Antichrist.[11] For some Americans, the year 2000 had an almost mystical quality about it, marking six thousand years since creation. Modelling human history on the pattern of the week described in Genesis 1-2, some argued that the six 'days' of world history were about to give way to a seventh 'day' of rest, a millennial peace that the year 2000 seemed to herald.[12] Others, equally driven by religious hope, were less benign, believing that God had called them to an active role in the realisation of his thousand years of millennial peace. Throughout the late 1990s, newspapers and magazines reported on the concerns of local authorities in Jerusalem. Israeli government officials were worried by the possibility that some of the religious groups that had recently moved to the area were intending to create conflict – in some cases, an apocalyptic conflict, they worried, designed to effect widespread panic and confusion. The authorities were concerned that these groups' religious hopes were designed as self-fulfilling prophecies. The extremists were attempting to use chaos in Jerusalem to generate a global conflict that, they hoped, would induce the second coming of Jesus and the institution of his earthly kingdom.[13] Christians and Muslims were using the apocalyptic literature of Scripture for totally different ends, but agreed that the near future involved the rise of violent and demonic persecution, and agreed that the conflict would centre on Jerusalem.[14] Their agreement was an ominous sign.

These apocalyptic fears shattered the uneasy peace that had emerged in the aftermath of the end of the Cold War. Throughout the 1990s, historians and political scientists had wondered whether the West might be approaching 'the end of history'. The expectation was grounded in the hope that the triumph of transnational capitalism marked the end of global conflict. The end of global conflict, it was believed, represented the virtual end of history, for Western, democratic, capitalist civilisation would continue without any other significant challenges. It was a good theory, reflecting a new sense of East-West détente, but it could not last. The complacency of many political scientists was shattered by the events of 11 September 2001, when Islamic terrorists, having hijacked several busy passenger planes, used them as guided missiles to attack the most celebrated symbols of American economic and military power. The thousands of resulting deaths drove those analysts seeking an understanding of world affairs back to a model of conflict. The new preference was for a model of 'civilizational' conflict, where international tensions were not simply caused by the differences between Communist East and Capitalist West, but between a host of social and cultural assumptions that flared most dangerously in those areas where these culturally-pervasive worldviews were seen to clash. The model seemed to be a perfect fit for the era of Balkans genocide, and *The End of History* was replaced by *The Clash of Civilisations*.[15] It became increasingly obvious that the European journey into a utopia after 'the end of history' had depended on American policy remaining firmly within 'history'; European peace was being constructed on American military power.[16] 'The end of history' was therefore a bankrupt hope.

No one could deny that world history since 9-11 has been dominated by concerns about terrorism and religiously-inspired violence. It seems as obvious in the videos of Osama bin Laden as in the patriotic rhetoric of President George W. Bush. He denies that his assault on the international 'axis of evil' is driven by his faith; but his state speeches habitually end with the famous appeal, 'God bless America.' Across the USA, voters anxiously interpret the events they watch on the news through a system of biblical interpretation whose dramatisation in the *Left Behind* novels looks more and more like an eerie prophecy of the present. For some, reality looks ever more like the events predicted in their favourite books.

There is something very disturbing about the way in which the modern world resembles the apocalyptic scenarios described in *Left Behind*. The series anticipated the divisions between the United Nations and the USA; 'old Europe' did seem to offer a threatening military alternative to the world's sole remaining super-power; and the series seemed correct in anticipating that the conflicts of the early twenty-first century would focus on Iraq. No wonder that sales of *Left Behind* surged after the attack on the World Trade Centre. The series' theology was reflecting – or, some have claimed, shaping – the policies of the Bush administration.[17] Whatever the truth, the world of rapture fiction has become the world of a terrible reality.

DISPENSATIONALISM

This converging of international politics and biblical analysis has become familiar to adherents of a system of evangelical theology known as 'dispensationalism'. This kind of theology – a variant of which is dramatised in the *Left Behind* series – was developed in the nineteenth century to argue that Jesus Christ could at any moment secretly return to 'rapture' to heaven all true believers, with everyone else left behind; that those left behind would enter a seven-year period known as the 'tribulation'; that, during the tribulation, a sinister dictator would rise to power to rule over a revived Roman Empire based in Europe; that this 'Antichrist' would mount the most savage persecution the world has ever seen; that this persecution would be focused on Jews, including those who have converted to the Christian faith and those Gentiles who have been persuaded by their evangelism; that this persecution would be made possible by the Antichrist's sophisticated use of innovative technology, which might include a technological 'mark of the beast'; and that his terrible regime would be ended by the second coming proper, when Jesus Christ would return with his people to defeat his enemies, bind the devil and establish his millennial kingdom of 1000 years. The end of the millennium would be followed by the final rebellion, the final battle, and the inauguration of the new heavens and earth.[18] The *Left Behind* novels dramatise one variant of this complex theology, and chart the fate of the 'tribulation force', a small band of those who come to faith after the rapture to face the consequences of Christian discipleship in a world governed by the most evil – and most powerful – man in history.

Dispensationalism – like other forms of Christian teaching about the end of all things – promotes a very black-and-white view of the world. Like the prophetic books of Daniel and Revelation, in which it bases many of its claims, dispensationalism argues that the on-going conflict between good and evil will ultimately result in the destruction of everything unrighteous. The most basic message of dispensationalism, like that of all other evangelical theologies of the end, is that Jesus Christ will return to earth as the Victor, completing the new creation that has begun in the salvation he has provided to his people. Those who have never committed their lives to him will be condemned eternally to hell. In that sense of moral judgement, dispensationalism is well within the orbit of traditional Christian orthodoxy.

But dispensationalism moves beyond what the church has always believed. In developing the idea that the rapture will occur before the tribulation, and by suggesting a period of history from which Christians will be removed, dispensationalism represents a real departure from the church's historic faith. This does not mean that it is wrong, merely innovative; but the novelty of dispensationalism is even more marked in the publications of those popular prophecy 'experts' who write their own political fears into their exegesis of biblical truth. A long line of prophecy 'experts' has found in Scripture all manner of references to the bogeymen of the present. Every anti-hero of the day has been written into the scenario of the end, from Cold War Communism to the increasingly powerful United Nations.[19] What these villains have in common is the danger to the American way of life they are believed to represent. In that sense, dispensationalism is a theology strongly inflected by fear. From the late nineteenth century to the present day, dispensationalism has articulated an ultimately American doomsday.

DISPENSATIONALISM AND AMERICAN CULTURE

The development of dispensationalism throughout the twentieth century has been profoundly marked by the American context of its most influential exponents. In concentrating on the biblical description of the end of the world, these leaders have not retreated into some unusual cultural backwater. From colonial times to the present day, American Protestantism has been deeply affected by a persistent interest in the end of the world.[20] America's earliest evangelical leaders published extensively on apocalyptic and millennial thought. Increase Mather, for example, built on the foundation of the earliest settlers to argue that Jesus Christ would return before the millennium (this has become known as 'pre-millennialism'). In the eighteenth century, Jonathan Edwards adopted certain aspects of the Enlightenment optimism of his day and argued from Scripture that Jesus Christ would return after the millennium (this has become known as 'post-millennialism'). Throughout the nineteenth century, American evangelicals continued to maintain both positions, with the theologians based in Princeton Seminary consolidating Presbyterianism's post-millennial expectations while others with equally evangelical credentials adhered to the several varieties of pre-millennialism that were evolving through the period. But the destruction of the First World War shattered the optimistic expectations of the evangelical post-millennialists, and a new generation of pre-millennial thinkers seized the initiative. In 1917 the Revd Cyrus Scofield published the second, and more popular, edition of the study Bible that was to make his name – and his theology – famous. Selling millions of copies, and with the kudos gained from being published by Oxford University Press, the *Scofield Reference Bible* was to dominate the apocalyptic thinking of several generations of American evangelicals, disseminating its innovative brand of dispensational and pre-millennial thought. Despite the rapid rise of a-millennialism – the belief that the thousand-year period described in Revelation 20 is a general symbol of all of the church age rather than a definite period in the future – pre-millennialism dominated the twentieth-century American imagination. Throughout evangelicalism were many whose 'hope was built on nothing less than Scofield's notes and Moody Press'.

By the mid-twentieth-century, dispensational pre-millennialism had become part of the American cultural mainstream, but its influence extended greatly after the 1970s. At the end of that decade, an estimated eight million Americans were 'firmly committed' to the variety of dispensationalism the novels advance.[21] Today, that number has multiplied. Two televangelists who share a commitment to the dispensational worldview, Pat Robertson and Jerry Falwell, claim to communicate with 100 million supporters every week.[22] Adherents of the dispensational worldview can be found throughout the entire spectrum of American life – and even in the Oval Office. Before his inauguration as President, Ronald Reagan stated his conviction that 'the day of Armageddon isn't far off ... Ezekiel says that fire and brimstone will be rained upon the enemies of God's people. That must mean that they'll be destroyed by nuclear weapons.'[23] Significantly, it was to the National Association of Evangelicals that President Reagan made his famous (and apocalyptic) reference to the 'evil empire' of Soviet Russia.[24] Several administrations later, at the beginning of the twenty-first century, supporters of dispensationalism have 'probably' become 'the most powerful lobby in the United States'.[25] A number of recent commentators have argued that their concerns pervade the theological interests and political policies of George W. Bush. In a Christmas 2004 'end of the world' special, *The Economist* reported fears that 'nutty, apocalyptic, born-again Texans are guiding not just conservative social policies at home, but America's agenda in the Middle East as well, as they round up reluctant

compatriots for the last battle at Armageddon'.[26] Dominating the
imaginations of successive Presidents, evangelical apocalypticism
has certainly come in from the cold.

With friends in high places and in low, the 'rapture' has become a central part of American folklore. The widespread appeal
of this system of theology has been signalled and consolidated
by the massive popularity of *Left Behind*. It has been a long time
since any evangelical author has been of sufficient public interest
to make the cover page of *TIME* or *Newsweek* – but, in the last
few years, Tim LaHaye and Jerry B. Jenkins have been featured on
both.[27] Their variant of dispensationalism – the ultimate American
nightmare – has been granted the ultimate American accolade.

RAPTURE FICTION AND PUBLIC CONTROVERSY

It is hardly surprising, therefore, that with widespread popular appeal and a stringent moral commitment, the *Left Behind* series has
made as many enemies as friends. Selling in venues as different
as Christian bookshops and airport terminals, the series has split
American popular opinion. An increasing number of newspaper
and magazine articles feature the authors, note the financial success the novels have provided, and systematically criticise their
political and cultural assumptions. Catholic leaders complain of
the series' overt Protestantism, and secularists complain of their
socially conservative opinions: why, they ask, should everyone except evangelicals be condemned to hell?[28]

No one is claiming that the novels are high art. The first major book-length study of the series complained that the novels'
characters 'seem flimsy and ill developed, the plot contrived, and
the writing thin'.[29] Other critics complain of the series' cultural
conservatism. Melani McAlister notes that although the novels
'claim to be about the future ... they are also very much about
the present'.[30] Amy Johnson Frykholm has agreed, finding in the
novels a 'conservative, patriarchal, even racist agenda that mirrors
that of the Christian Right'.[31] Elsewhere she complains of 'a strong
conservative agenda, a hostile antifeminist perspective, hints of
anti-Semitism, and an overt homophobia',[32] and quotes another

reviewer's description of the series as 'hard-core right-wing para-noid anti-Semitic homophobic misogynistic propaganda'.[33]

The reception has not been any warmer in the United King-dom, where the series has most often been discussed in connection with left-leaning European dissatisfaction with the foreign policy of the George W. Bush administration. From serious newspapers like *The Independent*, to serious literary reviews like *The Times Literary Supplement*, to mainstream television documentaries, the series has been repeatedly identified with all that European liberals find most objectionable about the American Christian Right.[34] There is a strong streak of snobbishness in many of the British reviews. Thank goodness, they seem to say, that audiences on our side of the Atlantic are too clever for this.

This snobbery is obvious in newspaper coverage in Britain. *The Times* described the *Left Behind* series as 'the oddest literary phenomenon in the English-speaking world ... Nostradamus re-written by Jeffrey Archer'.[35] *The Independent on Sunday* argued that the series' appeal is 'clearly bound up in class. Nobody with an educated view of either religion or literature would give it the time of day.'[36] The *Times Literary Supplement* reviewed *Glorious Appearing* (2004), the final novel in the initial twelve-volume series, and noted the 'awkwardness' with which its authors blended 'folksy humour, treacly sentiment and religiously justified bloodbaths'.[37] The series' plots offer 'very precise implications' for public policy, the *Times Literary Supplement* complained, for 'the God worshipped by LaHaye and Jenkins considers abortion to be wrong, has it in for gay people and feminists, and opposes most forms of govern-ment regulation, especially gun control.'[38] For its high-brow Brit-ish readers, the novels are simultaneously much too American and much too conservative to be models of good taste.

RAPTURE FICTION AND EVANGELICAL CONTROVERSY

But it would be a mistake for British audiences to assume that American conservatives have been uncritical of the series. Sev-enth-Day Adventists have argued that the series is too soft on Roman Catholicism, erring in its identification of the Antichrist, who, they claim, is obviously the Pope.[39] Catholic writers, sharing many of the series' ethical commitments, nevertheless complain that it is too hard on their communion.[40] Within evangelicalism, writers as diverse as confessional Presbyterians and non-confessional fundamentalists have complained of what they perceive to be the series' lack of biblical and theological caution.[41] At times they dismiss what they perceive to be its 'dramatic expression of … foolishness'.[42] At other times, they point to the series as a dramatic manifestation of Antichristian influence within the evangelical mainstream.[43] Nor have American evangelicals been slow to provide alternatives. Nathan D. Wilson has published a spoof that he has entitled *Right Behind: A Parody of Last Days Goofiness* (2001).[44] Hank Hanegraff, with greater seriousness, has published an alternative rapture novel, *The Last Disciples* (2004), which argues that the prophecies of Revelation refer to events at the end of the first century, rather than at the end of the age.[45] Even a number of leaders within dispensationalism have criticised the series for what they perceive to be a radical re-writing of the end.[46] In particular, as we will later see, they have insisted that those who have rejected the gospel in this age will not be granted a second chance of salvation in the tribulation, completely countering the series' most fundamental assumption. Strangely, therefore, despite its phenomenal success, the series is not at all representative of the mainstream dispensational tradition with which it is often identified.[47]

That dispensational mainstream has frequently been challenged by rapture fictions. Dispensational theology has been adapted into novels since World War One, and into films since the 1970s. Again and again, these fictions have focused on the spectacular impact of the rapture and the devastation and chaos of the tribulation. In showing their heroes coming to faith in Jesus Christ, they have made their agenda brilliantly clear: the only way a person can be saved from sin and assured of salvation is by grace alone, through faith alone, in Jesus Christ alone, to the glory of God alone. *Left Behind* has taken some of these central tenets of evangelicalism to a wider audience than ever before. Recent reading surveys indicate that the series has attracted a wider readership than any Christian novel series ever published. Almost one in every ten American adults has read at least one of the series.[48] And, almost certainly, many of those reading the novels for the first time believe that they are being exposed to an authentic and reliable exposition of the Christian faith. This book has been written with the concern that the series – like a great deal of evangelical rapture fiction more generally – may be a less reliable guide to the theology of the Bible than many millions of readers suppose.

Chapter 2

THE ORIGINS OF THE SECRET RAPTURE

'Clearly Bruce had been in tune with what God was showing him. He had said over and over that this was not new truth, that the commentaries he cited were decades old and that the doctrine of the end times was much, much older than that.'[1]

DIGITAL IMPLANTS, LEARJET GLOBETROTTING, and an internet church – the *Left Behind* novels are fashionably hip in their attitude to the modern world. The latest rapture fictions portray the immense technological power of the Antichrist, and the even greater technological power of those who would resist him. In *Nicolae* (1997), for example, Buck orders 'five of the absolute best, top-of-the-line computers, as small and compact as they can be, but with as much power and memory and speed and communications abilities as you can wire into them ... a computer with virtually no limitations'.[2] While these rapture novels emphasise the dangers of technological revolution, they are nevertheless excited by the possibilities it offers for believers. The series' fascination with technology almost overwhelms the characters' spiritual expectations: Chang thought it was ironic 'that with all the technology God had allowed them to adapt for the cause of Christ around the world, he was suddenly left with nothing to do to help, except old-fashioned praying'.[3] The *Left Behind* novels – like rapture fictions more generally – are infatuated by the most modern of gadgets.

This fascination with technology obscures the long historical roots of the rapture fiction genre. As we saw in the last chapter, the success of *Left Behind* and its modern counterparts was one expression of a more general rise of apocalyptic interest at the end of the twentieth century. We have also seen that rapture fiction has roots in the Protestant and evangelical tradition of end-time thinking, and specifically in the system of theology known as dispensational pre-millennialism. To understand the origins of the rapture fiction phenomenon, therefore, we need to go back to the beginning of the modern evangelical interest in the millennium, and the series of revolutions that threatened the stability of the eighteenth-century world.

DISPENSATIONALISM AND FEAR

At the end of the eighteenth century, Britain and its dominions were shaken by a series of revolutions that threatened to bring an end to the traditional political order. In 1776, the thirteen united American colonies issued their Declaration of Independence, denying the rights of the London Parliament to exercise authority in the New World, charging George III with 'absolute Tyranny' and announcing the dissolution of the 'political bands' which tied them to his rule. In 1789, France erupted in a revolution that threatened the political order of Europe. Widespread discussion of the 'rights of man' and the public execution of the French royal family encouraged democratic agitation across the continent and encouraged the formation of revolutionary societies within the British Isles. These radical tremors were felt closest to home in the 1790s, when Protestant political leaders in Ireland built on the central themes of the American and French revolutions to organise in support of parliamentary reform and to limit English influence in Irish political life. The leaders of the United Irishmen had expected military assistance from the French, but the latter's unsuccessful landing attempt in 1796 signalled the existence of the secret movement and led to its widespread suppression. In 1798, when the United Irishmen had over 280,000 active members, their grassroots support was developing a much more sectarian analysis of the Irish problem, and was organising for a national rising in late May. Plans for this island-wide revolution fell apart when the Dublin revolutionaries remained quiescent. The other risings – which had been planned as side-shows to the main event in the capital – were uncoordinated and, with the exception of those in Wexford and the north-east, failed to make much impact on the government. But the United Irishmen had demonstrated the danger of popular dissatisfaction with the Irish status quo.

As these revolutions more closely approached the British mainland, they generated increasing fear among those who had most to lose from the end of the existing social order. These fears were most concentrated in Ireland, where the Catholic population far outnumbered the Protestant middle and upper classes, and where the possible transference of political power threatened the very fabric of the established church and social order. For centuries, the families of the Irish Ascendancy, the Protestant ruling elite, had claimed political rights on the basis of conquest, and had rarely justified them in public service. At Trinity College, Dublin, where the sons of many of the elite families studied, academics grew increasingly concerned by the prospect of the resurgence of Catholic political violence and the possible end to the Ascendancy's comfortable status quo. Rebellion, they feared, would most likely bring democracy, and democracy spelled the end of their privilege. As the tumult of revolution echoed across Europe, it seemed as if their comfortable world was coming to an end.

In Ireland, these fears disturbed a number of prominent evangelical leaders, and drove them to search the prophetic Scriptures for hints of what was yet to come. In the context of political instability and threats of violence, these Dublin evangelicals turned back to consider the workings of God in history. At Trinity College, a number of prominent academics began to develop a reading of history that identified a series of distinctive, and divinely-controlled, periods.[4] These 'dispensations' provided a key to history which, they believed, heralded the final collapse of Roman Catholicism, the long-anticipated conversion of the Jews and their restoration to Palestine. The time was at hand, some of these academics were arguing; a change of dispensation was imminent, and the millennium was about to begin. Its peace would pave the way for the eventual coming of Jesus Christ.

The post-millennial theology of the Trinity College evangelicals was inherently conservative, emphasising the dangers both of popular democracy and any attempt to bring lower-class Catholics into the Irish political process. This post-millennialism was developed in order to consolidate existing structures of power in church and state. But there was a stirring of dissatisfaction among a small number of Trinity students and graduates. Concerned by the conservative political implications and uncertain biblical foundations of this post-millennial vision, they returned to Scripture study and developed a theological system that would challenge the assumptions of the establishment at its very foundation. Their revival of interest in the millennium created the environment in which a renewed pre-millennialism, and a new kind of dispensationalism, would flourish.

Pre-millennial dispensationalism was developed in the 1820s and 1830s by a small group of conservative evangelicals associated with Trinity College and the emerging 'Plymouth' Brethren.[5] One of the most prominent of this group, John Nelson Darby (1800-1882), openly admitted the impact on his theology of Ireland's sudden political change:

> I, a conservative by birth, by education and by mind; a
> Protestant in Ireland into the bargain; I had been moved

to the very depths of my soul on seeing that everything
was going to be shaken. The testimony of God made me
see and feel that all should be shaken, but ... that we have
a kingdom that cannot be shaken.[6]

Darby's interest in biblical prophecy was at least partly stimulated by his sense that his privileged world was coming to an
end.[7]

And Darby's background was certainly privileged. His family had impeccable social credentials, combining English business
success and American political connections with the status of Irish
landed gentry. The Darby family owned Leap Castle in county
Offaly, though Darby's father, as a younger son, had chosen to
pursue a business career in London. Darby's father, who was also
called John (1751-1834), inherited the estate after the death of his
older brother, Admiral Sir Henry D'Esterre Darby, who had served
under Lord Nelson (after whom John Nelson Darby was named).
John Darby had established his fortunes through a series of prof-
itable government contracts developed during the Napoleonic
Wars. Through business, he had come into contact with Samuel
Vaughan, an American businessman with important political
connections. Vaughan owned a number of sugar plantations in
Jamaica and large estates in Maine, numbered George Washington
among his friends, and had been entrusted with the landscaping
of Independence Square in Philadelphia. Vaughan's sons were active in the pursuit of new learning and American liberty. William
was in business in London, a Fellow of the Royal Society, and the
founder of the first savings bank in 1815. Samuel junior had a
keen interest in American political life, reporting the development
of the emerging constitution and developing plans to support the
currency of the US Mint through geological exploration. John was
Treasurer and Librarian of the American Philosophical Society for
four decades while running a successful wine business. The eldest
of the Vaughan brothers, Benjamin, was the most prominent of
this remarkable family. He was a friend of Benjamin Franklin and
a provider of 'crucial assistance' in the peace negotiations at the
end of the War of Independence in 1783. But it was Vaughan's

daughter, Ann (d. 1847), who caught John Darby's eye and became his wife in 1784. The marriage secured the Irish family's links with one of the most prestigious and patriotic of American families when they seemed to be at the height of their influence.

But there were problems. The Darbys were Anglican, while the Vaughans were Unitarian. Ann's oldest brothers had attended Warrington Academy, and the freethinkers Jeremy Bentham and Joseph Priestley, who had taught there, were among the family's friends. Although we have little evidence either way, it is likely that Ann Vaughan, after her wedding, fell in with the Darby family's faith. She provided her husband with several children. John Nelson Darby, their youngest, was born in 1800.

Darby's early life seems to have been unspectacular. He was educated at Westminster School, London, before moving to Trinity College, Dublin, in 1815, where he graduated with high honours and a coveted Gold Medal in Classics in 1819. In the same year he was admitted to Lincoln's Inn, London, and, in 1822, to the Irish bar. His brother-in-law, Edward Pennefather, was already established in legal circles, and was later to become Lord Chief Justice of Ireland. But Darby was unsatisfied by the promise of a successful legal career, worrying that 'he should be selling his services to defeat justice':[8]

> I was a lawyer; but feeling that, if the Son of God gave Himself for me I owed myself entirely to Him, and that the so-called christian world was characterised by deep ingratitude towards Him, I longed for complete devotedness to the work of the Lord, my chief thought was to get round amongst the poor Catholics of Ireland. I was induced to be ordained.[9]

Much to the consternation of his father, Darby abandoned his legal training, and, in 1825, was ordained as a deacon in the Church of Ireland.

Darby quickly established a reputation for hard pastoral work. From a rural base in Calary, county Wicklow, Darby trekked the hills, visiting the Catholic peasantry in remote houses and speaking to them about the salvation offered by Jesus Christ: 'As soon as I was ordained, I went amongst the poor Irish mountaineers, in a wild and uncultivated district, where I remained two years and three months, working as best I could.'[10] Francis Newman, an early observer, described Darby in this period as

> an indefatigable curate in the mountains of Wicklow. Every evening he sallied forth to teach in the cabins, and roving far and wide over mountain and amid bogs, was seldom home before midnight. By such exertions his strength was undermined ... He did not fast on purpose, but his long walks through wild country and indigent people inflicted on him much severe deprivation: moreover, he ate whatever food offered itself – food unpalatable and often indigestible to him – his whole frame might have vied in emaciation with a monk of La Trappe.
>
> Such a phenomenon intensely excited the poor Romanists, who looked on him as a genuine "saint" of the ancient breed. The stamp of heaven seemed to them clear in a frame so wasted by austerity, so superior to worldly pomp, and so partaking in all their indigence. That a dozen such men would have done more to convert all Ireland to Protestantism, than the whole apparatus of the Church Establishment, was ere long my conviction.[11]

What is perhaps most significant about Newman's statement is that it describes the work that Darby engaged in before his conversion to evangelicalism: 'not yet knowing deliverance, I was governed by the feeling of duty towards Christ, rather than by the consciousness that *He* had done *all* and that I was redeemed and saved'.[12]

But that knowledge of salvation was swiftly granted. Francis Newman was a tutor in the Pennefather home, and met Darby when he came to the household to recuperate after a debilitating riding accident, in the winter of 1827-28. It was during that period of recuperation that Darby began to realize the implications of the Christian's union with Christ. Many years later, Darby remembered that

> I was troubled ... when a clergyman ... going from cabin
> to cabin to speak of Christ, and with souls, these thoughts
> sprang up, and if I sought to quote a text to myself it
> seemed a shadow and not real. I ought never to have been
> there ... I was not set free according to Romans viii.[13]

But, that winter in the Pennefather household, Darby found himself released from this intense conviction of sin into the liberty of a realized union with Jesus Christ. In later years, Darby looked back on these events in the winter of 1827-28 as the time when he first knew assurance of salvation. It was, perhaps, the moment he became an evangelical.

Darby's years as an 'indefatigable curate', prior to his evangelical conversion, illustrate the depth of his adherence to an almost Catholic system of theology. Remembering these years of spiritual conflict and doubt, Darby later admitted that he 'thought much of Rome, and its professed sanctity, and catholicity, and antiquity ... Protestantism met none of these feelings'.[14] Adopting an extremely high churchmanship, Darby

> fasted in Lent so as to be weak in body at the end of it; ate
> no meat on week days – nothing till evening on Wednesdays, Fridays, and Saturdays, then a little bread or nothing; observed strictly the weekly fasts, too. I went to my
> clergyman always if I wished to take the sacrament that
> he might judge of the matter. I held apostolic succession
> fully, and the channels of grace to be there only. I held
> thus Luther and Calvin and their followers to be outside.
> I was not their judge, but I left them to the uncovenanted
> mercies of God.[15]

Remarkably, it was during this time of high churchmanship – which shut the followers of Luther and Calvin outside the covenanted mercies of God – that Darby's mind turned towards the study of the millennium.

THE EMERGENCE OF THE SECRET RAPTURE

The study of the origins of the secret rapture, and the two-stage coming of Christ, has developed in certain circles into something of a cottage industry. Over the years, Dave MacPherson has argued in a series of publications that the doctrine was first propounded in an ecstatic utterance during one of the first recorded examples of modern Pentecostal phenomena, when a prophecy by Margaret Macdonald purportedly suggested that a secret coming of Christ would precede his coming in glory.[16] Others have used this evidence to claim that the secret rapture owes its origins to the occult.[17] Recent evidence suggests, however, that Darby was acquainted with the idea at least several months before Macdonald's utterance. It is possible that Darby's interest in the millennium was stimulated by his pre-evangelical interest in Roman Catholicism, and, more specifically, it is possible that he discovered the idea of a secret rapture and two-stage second coming from Catholic sources during a visit to France.

Darby travelled to Paris in 1830, perhaps at the same time as his friend Lady Powerscourt and the Revd Robert Daly, Darby's rector and Lady Powerscourt's minister. Darby left no record of this expedition, though it has been documented from other sources in Brethren history, so it is impossible to exactly list his contacts. Robert Daly, on the other hand, provided a detailed account of his visit to the city, and it is likely that Darby, as another Irish Protestant, would have shared his excitement in learning of the existence of a number of religious communities committed to the reformation of Roman Catholicism. Daly noted that the Jansenists 'knew the truth, and, though they held many Roman Catholic errors, rejoiced in hearing the doctrines of grace'.[18]

In a recent publication, the historian Timothy C. F. Stunt has suggested that the Parisian Jansenists provided a model for Darby's end-time thinking.[19] With their careful and unvarnished devotion to the traditional Catholic faith, the Jansenists were appalled by the events of the 1790s: the revolution was destroying churches at the same time as the Catholic hierarchy were offering concessions to the new regime. Horrified by the condition of France, the Jansenists increasingly turned their attention to apocalyptic themes, expecting to witness the Jews' return to Palestine and the beginning of the last days. One of the most significant Jansenist theologians was the Dominican Bernard Lambert (1738-1813), whose apocalyptic interests were shared by a Parisian lawyer, Pierre-Jean Agier (1748-1823). Both men began a voluminous – if somewhat marginal – publishing campaign.

There is some evidence that the work of Lambert and Agier was being read alongside the more popular work of Manuel Lacunza, a Jesuit writer whose anonymous publications were advancing a form of pre-millennialism that was to appeal to the Revd Edward Irving (1792-1834). Irving was a Scottish Presbyterian minister whose fashionable ministry in London was attracting a great deal of critical attention, not least because of his expulsion from the Church of Scotland in 1831 on the charge of heresy. Irving was fascinated by the end of the world, and republished Lacunza's work in English to popularise his increasingly pre-millennial commitment. Helped by these links with Irving, Lacunza's work was widely received. But there was at least one significant difference between the work of Lacunza and that of the two Parisian Jansenists. Lacunza argued that Christ would return once, at the beginning of the millennium; Lambert, on the other hand, argued that Christ would return twice, once to gather his saints, and then again, at the beginning of the millennium, to reign. This distinction was to be of vast importance. Several years before the idea was popularised by Darby and the Brethren, Father Lambert was teaching a secret, pre-millennial, rapture.

What is certain, therefore, is that the idea of a two-stage second coming was circulating some time before Darby heard Margaret Macdonald's ecstatic utterance in autumn 1830, and it is possible, given the details of his visit to Paris, that Darby may have come into contact with its exponents. Darby certainly recognised the value of their work. In the 1850s, Samuel Prideaux

Tregelles, a Brethren textual scholar, remembered that 'Lambert and Agier were the writers Mr. J. N. Darby studied earnestly before he left the Church of England. I remember his speaking much about them in 1835.'[20] It is important to realise, therefore, that the two-stage second coming existed before it was popularised by Darby, and that it was developed and then disseminated in times of political crisis. Whether in revolutionary France or revolutionary Ireland, the two-stage second coming, centred on the concept of the secret rapture, developed to reflect its adherents' concern about the end of an existing social order, and the threat it posed to an established church.

So how did a theory that Darby may first have heard on a visit to Paris develop into the theological system that would come to dominate modern American evangelicalism? The answer is complex – and simple. Dispensationalism developed among the early Brethren in Dublin; was refined in discussions at the conferences of evangelical leaders at Albury in Surrey and Powerscourt in county Wicklow; and was most clearly outlined by Darby in a series of lectures in Lausanne in the 1840s. Thereafter, the new interpretation began to spread rapidly among the clergy of the established churches, being popularised in magazines and the series of societies established to foster the study of Biblical prophecy. After his mother's death, Darby began his series of journeys to North America, where a form of dispensationalism stripped of his Calvinism and ecclesiastical separatism gripped the evangelical imagination, and established itself as the new orthodox creed of emerging fundamentalists.[21]

The dispensational rapture has moved far from these Calvinist beginnings. Those beginnings are perhaps surprising: Darby's strong Calvinism has been underplayed, both within dispensational circles and among their most vociferous critics. Yet in North America, as in England and Ireland, Darby's dispensationalism developed most extensively among traditionally Reformed communities. Its earliest and most vigorous exponents were Presbyterians, though it was a Congregational minister, the Revd C. I. Scofield, who gave his name to the most celebrated of dispensational study Bibles.[22] With the rise of Protestant fundamentalism in the early twentieth century, Scofield's dispensationalism became a part of a besieged orthodoxy, then, with the rising influence of Billy Graham in the middle of the twentieth century, part of a new and more confident evangelical resurgence that downplayed certain elements of the earlier worldview. During the Cold War, however, North American evangelicalism returned to its sense of apocalyptic imminence. But as it did so, it echoed the interests of Jansenists in revolutionary France, and the emerging Brethren in revolutionary Ireland. Facing challenges to the traditional orders in church and state, overwhelmed by the threats of a hostile world, and concerned by the failures of their church, French Jansenists, Irish Brethren, and American evangelicals turned to embrace the hope that they would be removed from the earth before the impact of the worst. Today, it is estimated, tens of millions of Americans adhere to the system of theology Darby disseminated. Father Bernard could never have anticipated its appeal. In *Left Behind*, the ideas of a forgotten Parisian theologian may be addressing a wider audience than ever before.

DISPENSATIONAL CHANGES

Of course, the fact that the secret rapture emerged from the Parisian Catholic underground does not imply that modern premillennial dispensationalism is an inherently Catholic theology – despite the claims of certain of its critics. The fact that so many of its references to Catholicism are critical suggests that its sympathies could hardly be so understood. But dispensationalism has passed through a number of crucial changes as it has moved from the margins to the centre of North American evangelical life. By far the most serious of these changes has been its varying presentation of the gospel.

Although Darby began his investigation of prophecy while still under the influence of high Anglican theology, his evangelical conversion turned him into an emphatically Protestant theologian. The 'present system of Romanism', he claimed, has connected 'the claims and privileges of Christianity with the most constant opposition to its truth, its spirit, and its practice'.[23] 'Popery', he continued elsewhere, is associated with 'the worst form of evil under the sun'.[24] The contrast between these statements and those of the most influential modern dispensationalists is striking. In *Left Behind*, these older evangelical attitudes towards Roman Catholicism have been completely re-written. Darby would have been astonished to discover that his successors could imagine the Pope being among those taken at the rapture. Throughout the series, we can find many similar examples of the distance that modern dispensationalism has moved from the opinions of those who first advanced its claims.

The recognition of these kinds of contrast should not imply that there is, or ever has been, a single dispensational system of theology. Dispensationalism is a movement that lacks a common, defined confession of faith. Theologians who share a dispensational eschatological viewpoint can adopt contradictory attitudes to other aspects of Christian thought. It is this variety of dispensational opinions that makes it easy for some of the movement's critics to quote the opinions of eccentric extremists while assuming that they represent 'the dispensational view'. Dispensationalism shares the sense of variety that is present in many other forms of evangelical thought. As in many other schools of thought, there are probably as many dispensational views of salvation as there are dispensational theologians.

But this recognition of theological variety does not conflict with the basic theme for which this book contends. Dispensationalism, as represented in some of the best-selling novels of the twenty-first century, is strangely different from the system of theology that emerged from the Irish political crisis of the 1820s and 1830s. Dispensationalism has changed – changed for the worse – and is now exemplifying the most serious symptoms of the twenty-first century evangelical crisis.

DISPENSATIONAL DEBATE

Within the evangelical world, the growth of dispensationalism has caused as much concern as celebration. That concern is evident in the long series of refutations that have addressed the influence of the movement. Reformed theologians, in particular, have expressed concern at what they perceive to be the movement's shaky biblical foundations. Any analysis of the literature of this debate will show that writers on both sides tend to repeat the same charges and allegations, and often seem to be more familiar with their own side's summary of their opponents than with the actual claims of those with whom they disagree.

Classical dispensational theology is not nearly as dangerous as many of its critics believe. Of course, there are often differences between the dispensationalism of extremists and the dispensationalism of careful theologians: few dispensational theologians would agree with Peter Ruckman's statement that those 'left behind' should 'start working like a madman to get to heaven, because you're going to have to … the plan of salvation in the Tribulation is faith in Jesus Christ plus your good works.'[25] Mainstream dispensationalists would properly dismiss this as nonsense. Charles Ryrie's *Dispensationalism Today* (1965) is a good reflection of this mainstream opinion, and, despite its age, the book contains much that is relevant to contemporary discussions. Ryrie lists the areas of concern which Reformed (or 'covenant') theologians have frequently raised against dispensationalism – for example, its recent origins, its deductive approach, its hermeneutical straight-jacket, and its suggestion of salvation by law – and turns these familiar arguments on their heads. Ryrie volleys a series of counterclaims which attempt to undercut much of the high ground which covenant theologians have assumed. He argues, for example, that many of these same charges can be raised against covenant theology itself. As a system, he claims, it is 'not any older than dispensationalism'.[26] It is 'not the theology of the Reformers'.[27] And, just as dispensational writings can be manipulated to imply two ways of salvation, so Ryrie manipulates the data to make the daring (but surely tongue-in-cheek) suggestion that 'covenant theology must be teaching two ways of salvation – one by law and one by grace!'[28] Thus he concludes: 'The things which are charged against dispensationalism can be charged with equal justice against covenant theology … If these matters are not relevant to covenant theology, then covenant writers would do well to stop trying to make so much of them in their attacks on dispensationalism.'[29]

Ryrie makes a number of excellent points, but several recent critiques of dispensationalism do not appear to heed his advice. Robert Reymond's *Systematic Theology* (1998) claimed that dispensationalists 'differ widely among themselves over how many ... dispensations there are'. This claim seriously underplays the consensus of academic dispensational theologians, and gives too much credibility to the voices of those who are least broadly respected.[30] Similarly, and more seriously, in his charge that dispensationalists teach '*at least two* different plans of salvation in Scripture', Reymond's fine volume overlooks the patient qualifications which leading dispensational academics have so often made.[31] Ryrie has gone on record to insist that 'the *basis* of salvation in every dispensation is the death of Christ; the requirement for salvation in every age is faith; the object of faith is the true God; but the content of faith changes in the various dispensations.'[32] Others have paid heed. A. A. Hoekema, in his a-millennial textbook *The Bible and the Future* (1979), expressed his 'appreciation' for the statement made by the editors of the *New Scofield Reference Bible* (1967) that 'in each dispensation there is only one basis for salvation: by God's grace through the work of Christ accomplished on the cross and vindicated in his resurrection.'[33] O. Palmer Robertson has also thanked dispensationalists for this clarification.[34] But it seems that not all covenant theologians are paying attention. This book does not dispute that dispensational theologians teach the existence of only one way of salvation – but it does take serious issue with what the best-selling contemporary representatives of dispensationalism believe that way of salvation should involve.

This focus on the gospel is of paramount importance. In the last few years, however, the debate about dispensationalism has moved to different ground as controversial writing has focused on its cultural effects. A series of publications have exercised massive influence among those evangelicals concerned by the movement's lack of significant cultural impact. Mark Noll, Alister McGrath and Os Guinness have each asserted that the 'scandal of the evangelical mind' – evangelicalism's apparently anti-intellectual bias – has been fostered by the obscurantism of early twentieth-century fundamentalism, an obscurantism, they argue, which has been generated by fundamentalism's commitment to dispensational thought.[35]

There is weight in many of their charges, but this book argues, instead, that the cultural weakness of so much modern evangelicalism is not primarily due to its convictions about the end of the world, or how those convictions impact the Christian's daily life, or his relation to wider culture, important though these themes are. These issues are serious, and worthy of consideration, but they are not central. Instead, this book argues that the 'scandal of the evangelical mind' is actually the scandal of the evangelical gospel, and that the weakness of modern evangelicalism should instead be traced to its increasing confusion about the contents of the gospel message, the role of the church and its ordinances, the downplaying of the centrality of Scripture, and the elevation of the individual above the church fellowship. This is not merely a criticism of dispensationalism – it is a recognition that modern evangelicalism has entered a time of serious crisis, and that dispensational writings increasingly reflect that wider malaise.

The crisis might well have been anticipated by Darby and the other early Brethren, with their expectation of apostasy and ecclesiastical decay. But this chapter's account of the French origins of dispensationalism demonstrates that the idea of the secret rapture is not inherently linked to an evangelical understanding of the gospel. Nevertheless, the chapter has also argued that, through the influence of Darby and other Brethren leaders, early dispensationalism was quickly combined with an evangelical understanding of the gospel. The problem is that the *Left Behind* novels are un-doing Darby's work by prising the rapture apart from the gospel and pushing the rapture back into its pre-evangelical confusion.

The *Left Behind* novels claim that their version of dispensationalism has roots deep in Christian history. 'Bruce ... said over and over that this was not new truth, that the commentaries he cited were decades old and that the doctrine of the end times was much, much older than that.'[36] If only his understanding of the gospel were too.

Chapter 3

THE ORIGINS OF RAPTURE FICTION

'Nothing could have been scripted like this, Buck thought, blinking slowly. If somebody tried to sell a screenplay about millions of people disappearing, leaving everything but their bodies behind, it would be laughed off.'[1]

Until the mid-1990s, the book that people were most likely to think of when they thought about dispensationalism was Hal Lindsey's *The Late Great Planet Earth* (1970).[2] Lindsey's dispensational sensationalism was the best-selling 'non-fiction' book of the 1970s, selling over four million copies in the first four years of its publication before going on to sell some twenty million copies in translation. With maps and charts diagramming its basic themes, *The Late Great Planet Earth* interpreted some central dispensational themes for an audience worried by the Cold War. At the same time, however, Lindsey's book subtly challenged the dispensational consensus by making some prophetic claims of its own. Lindsey believed in making the biblical prophecies relate to the modern world. Adopting a form of 'exegesis by current events', Lindsey appeared to abandon the dispensational preference for the literal interpretation of Scripture, and discovered attack helicopters in biblical descriptions of locusts, and pilots' helmets in references to 'crowns of gold'.[3] At the height of the Cold War, his arguments entered deep into the American psyche. Lindsey's analysis was attractive to people in many prominent positions of power – President Ronald Reagan was perhaps his most famous disciple – and it appears that his combination of prophetic curiosity and political concern generated significant interest in some of the highest centres of the American military.[4] Trading on his reputation, Lindsey invested his new-found political capital and, for a time, provided advice to the Pentagon. But he was as active in finding a popular audience. Lindsey filled his books with puns and humour, and had Orson Welles narrate a film adaptation of *The Late Great Planet Earth* in 1978. His work was driving popular prophecy writing towards the edge of entertainment. The boundaries were finally blurred in 1996, when he published his own rapture novel, *Blood Moon*. *The Late Great Planet Earth* had created the conditions for the success of several different rapture fictions, and Lindsey didn't want to be left behind.

THE ORIGINS OF RAPTURE FICTION

Hal Lindsey's combination of dispensational theology and accessible literary style was clearly designed to take his ideas to as wide an audience as possible. With all its talk of doom and gloom, it has often been difficult to market apocalyptic thinking. Since the beginning of the twentieth century, therefore, Christian writers have repeatedly turned to fiction as a means to communicate their ideas.

The most successful of the early rapture novelists was Sydney Watson. He may not have been the father of the genre – rapture fictions from as early as 1905 have been identified[5] – but

Watson's work has certainly been kept in print over most of the last century. Watson was an established Christian writer before he turned his attention to promoting his understanding of end-times theology in novels such as *Scarlet and Purple* (1913), *The Mark of the Beast* (1915), and *In the Twinkling of an Eye* (1916).[6] In the situation his novels reflect, evangelical study of prophecy was burgeoning: there are now 'myriads' of prophetic study books, according to one of his characters.[7] But despite the popularity of his subject matter, Watson felt the need to defend his decision to use fiction: 'The first and only real problem I had to face in the matter was that of the principle involved in using the fictional form to clothe so sacred a subject', he claimed.[8] Perhaps not all of his readers were so easily convinced. The preface to the second novel of the series continued to defend the fictional mode by appealing to a policy of theological pragmatism, asserting that 'many thousands have read, and have been awakened, quickened, even converted' by the first novel and other evangelistic fictions.[9] Citing divine utility ('how wondrously God had owned and blessed' another example of Christian fiction) and the example of the parables (a book 'written in the vein our Lord himself suggests … could not have been written in any other way'), Watson established the basic contours and the stock characters and events of the rapture fiction genre.[10]

The main character in the first novel, *In the Twinkling of an Eye*, is a thirty-year old bachelor, a journalist named Tom Hammond.[11] Facing unexpected unemployment, he is given the opportunity to launch a new daily newspaper, which rapidly becomes the most successful newspaper in the world.[12] One of the paper's features is a daily column, which Hammond writes, entitled 'From the Prophet's Chair': 'every editor,' Hammond notes, 'ought to have a strain of the seer'.[13] Despite his interest in biblical prophecy and the political aspects of the early twentieth century 'Jewish problem', Hammond only slowly comes to embrace evangelical faith. His spiritual interests are quickened through his attending a number of afternoon lectures on biblical prophecy and through his increasingly romantic relationship with Zillah Robart, a Jewess associated with a scheme to rebuild the Temple in Jerusalem. The novel argues that 'the first sign of [Christ's] return is an awakening of national life among the Jews, that shall immediately precede their return – in unbelief – to their own land.'[14] Watson's series consolidated the genre's interest in the Jewish people and the Jewish state.

Although the novels are optimistic about the 'Jewish problem', they reiterate the social pessimism of the early twentieth-century pre-millennialists: 'The Bible nowhere gives a hint that the world is to be converted before the return of the Lord for His Church,' one preacher states in a didactic passage in the trilogy's final instalment, *In the Twinkling of an Eye*; 'as a matter of fact, the world – the times – are to grow worse and worse; more polished, more cultured, cleverer, better educated, yet grosser in soul, falser in worship.'[15] This pessimism shapes Hammond's concern about the small numbers of those likely to be involved in the rapture:

> 'If Christ came this instant,' he mused, 'how many of those Commoners and Peers would be ready to meet Him? And what of the teeming millions of this mighty city? God help us all! What blind fools we are!'[16]

Like the evangelical leaders of the nineteenth century, Watson's novels are concerned by urban deprivation and industrial squalor. London is described as a 'mighty Babylon' of vice and misery, where, after the rapture, 'the hordes of the vicious that festered in the slums' could creep from their 'filthy lairs' to become a 'menace to public life and property'.[17] There is a hint, too, of social critique in the narrative's note that 'Hell had no shadow of terror to people who, for years, had suffered the torments of a life in a literal hell in London.'[18] Unlike the evangelical leaders of the nineteenth century, however, Watson's novels propose no remedy for the tensions of urbanisation; the rapture is the only answer to the degeneration of society.

The rapture is also presented as the only remedy to problems in the church. The novels complain that lower standards of holiness were crippling the church. 'Certain religious and semi-religious journals', for example, discussed whether '*true* Christians could attend the Theatre and Music-Hall', but the fact that no one from 'these London houses of amusement' was involved in the rapture answered that question 'as it has never been answered before'.[19] Perhaps more serious were the explicit denials of historic orthodoxy tolerated in the name of theological Modernism: 'in the early part of the first decade of the twentieth century, men calling themselves Christians, taking the salaries of Christian ministers, openly denied every fundamental truth of the Bible – Sin, the Fall, The Atonement, The Resurrection, the Immaculate Birth of Christ, His Deity, the Personality of Satan, the Personality of the Holy Spirit, and everything else in God's Word which clashed with the flesh of their unregenerate lives.'[20] This downgrade in doctrine was accompanied by the lessening of commitment to denominational distinctives, as ecumenism fostered changes in historical hymnody and tinkered with traditional liturgical texts.[21] Worse, still, was the Modernist abuse of the Bible. Higher critics had brought about a 'gradual decay of reverence for the Word of God', the novel complained; these were 'men who broke Spurgeon's heart'.[22]

Watson's novels therefore emerge from an English evangelicalism that, at the beginning of the twentieth century, retained the social concern – if not the reforming vision – of the nineteenth-century evangelical reformers while beginning to define itself in opposition to the theological mainstream. The novels identify their heroes as 'ultra-Protestants' adhering to a 'Moody and Sankey religion'.[23] But this evangelicalism is careful not to identify itself with any particular denomination. Such identification is made impossible by the extent of ecclesiastical decay. 'The Devil is a Ritualist,' but the sacramentalism of the establishment 'finds its parallel in the Rationalism, Unitarianism, Socialism, etc., of Nonconformity'.[24] Naturally, Roman Catholicism is vilified, and those 'ultra-Protestants' who resist her claims are patriots as well as puritans: 'Romanism boldly declares its aim to win, or coerce Britain back into her harlot fold.'[25] Adhering to a long Protestant convention, Watson's 'Romanism' is the apocalyptic beast, which had deliberately played down the eschatological consciousness of the early church fathers to stifle any recognition of her diabolic role in the latter times: 'as Roman Papal Catholicism advanced, the looking for Christ's return died down.'[26]

The churches can therefore offer no solution to the decline of Christianity. Watson's novels imagine the pre-rapture faithful being led not by clergy but by the kind of respectable middle-class laity that had emerged to lead the Brethren movement and organise the interdenominational prophetic conferences. Conventional leadership roles are attributed to 'a well-known military officer, a writer on prophecy' and 'a well-known West End Christian doctor', but, as in other cultures of radical religion, Watson's prophetic movement also offered opportunities for female leadership.[27] Not many clergy would be raptured, and their failure to understand either the evangelical gospel or dispensational pre-millennialism would become one of the distinctive themes of the genre; their post-rapture public confessions would emphasise the importance of prophetic knowledge and evangelical conversion.[28] *The Mark of the Beast*, for example, was dedicated to the Revd G. Campbell Morgan, pulpit hero of London evangelicalism in the early decades of the twentieth century; but even then, on the first Sunday after the rapture, when Ralph Bastin goes to 'a great Nonconformist church where one of London's most popular and remarkable preachers had ministered', he is surprised to discover that the church secretary has been left behind, even though his wife and daughter were taken.[29] Future writers would elaborate the theme.

The novels are also pessimistic about the political future, and Watson's novels echo the concerns of the series' middle-class readers. Despite Hammond's growing interest in Judaism and his romance with Zillah Robart, the novels' depictions of the tribulation dramatise the fears of Jewish internationalism and worldwide economic conspiracy that were so current in certain early twentieth-century elites.[30] Following a long exegetical tradition, Watson's novels present the Antichrist as a Jew; Watson thanks Campbell Morgan for the idea that the Antichrist would be a reincarnation of Judas Iscariot.[31] Antichrist's rule would undercut the distinctive political identity of Britain. Although 'the peoples of all the world' associated Britain with the 'two thoughts of safety and liberty', the onset of the tribulation would put the British throne 'under the supreme rule of a Jew' whose empire would be governed from his capital in Babylon.[32] Because his empire would be limited to the actual territory the Romans controlled, Ireland would necessarily gain home rule and, to fulfil other biblical prophecies, Jews would return to control the land of Palestine.[33]

The tribulation's changing political paradigm would be accompanied by religious and moral collapse. Women would almost universally take up smoking and marriage would be scorned, while the religious world would continue its drive towards a one-world religion mixing 'Romanism, Spiritism (demonology), Theosophy, Materialism and other kindred cults' with liturgical music of a 'sensuous, voluptuous character'.[34] It is against a background of this idolatry that the Antichrist would take revenge on those whom the rapture had left behind who had since adopted the evangelical faith. Watson echoes the writings of the Reformation, recounting the 'trio of Protestants' being taken 'up the steps of the scaffold' to be beheaded.[35] The link between Antichrist and the guillotine – emerging from the evangelical response to French revolutionary terror, echoed here, in successive rapture films and in Jenkins' and La Haye's *The Mark* (2000) – is explicit: 'let's call a blade a blade'.[36] The question continually posed by Watson's novels therefore has more than theological overtones: 'Think of what it will mean, unsaved friend, if you are ... Left! Left behind!'[37]

Re-writing the rapture

There can be little doubt that Watson's legacy overshadows much of the subsequent development of the rapture novel genre. This was evident at the height of the Cold War, when one-time director of the UK Atomic Energy Authority, Dr Frederick A. Tatford, noted the appeal of Watson's fiction in the preface to his own rapture novel, *The Clock Strikes* (1971).[38] Tatford acknowledged that his novel would not replace Watson's fiction; *The Clock Strikes* would be 'on similar lines to *The Mark of the Beast*, but with a somewhat more modern setting'.[39] But as the rapture was re-written, it was made to conform to a stricter dispensationalism;

with his references to Spurgeon, Moody and Sankey, Watson was drawing on a wider evangelical tradition than Tatford or later rapture writers. Despite this increased complexity, Tatford's novel refused to echo the didactic detail that had by then come to typify the genre: 'Those who come to this book, expecting to find a precise outline of the Bible's teaching on prophecy will be disappointed. One has attempted to do that in other books which are available.'[40] Nevertheless, Tatford's writing was clearly purposeful, and had to take account of the fact that some events that Watson had relegated to the tribulation – such as the re-birth of Israel – had already taken place. Tatford's novel therefore emphasised the importance of 'topical subjects and developments', including the evolution of the European Common Market and the significance of the ecumenical movement in the preparations for a one-world religion.[41] *The Clock Strikes* was a spirited attempt to update the rapture fiction genre to take account of the realities of the Cold War, following the outline of future military events provided one year earlier by *The Late Great Planet Earth*. His efforts went hand-in-hand with Salem Kirban's two rapture fictions, *666* (1970) and *1000* (1973), and the series of rapture movies directed by Donald W. Thompson, following the immensely successful *A Thief in the Night* (1972), *A Distant Thunder* (1978), *Image of the Beast* (1980), and *The Prodigal Planet* (1983).

By the 1990s, however, a more radical reinvention was re-quired to take account of the collapse of the Cold War and the dramatic reversal of popular dispensational expectations. The USSR was no longer America's apocalyptic enemy; now the threat of rogue states and the dangers of a 'new world order' challenged those commentators who still pointed to Russia's role in the fulfil-ment of Biblical prophecy. Throughout the 1990s, dispensational exegetes revised the prophetic future to take account of current concerns. This radical restructuring of the prophetic worldview is what makes the work of Jenkins and LaHaye most interesting.

Left Behind (1995) is taut and frantic. It documents the initial impact of the rapture and introduces central characters as they re-spond to the sudden disappearance of one-third of the passengers on the aircraft on which they are travelling. Despite its apparent novelty, *Left Behind* is profoundly conscious of its genre. This is evident, for example, in its developing one of the genre's stock characters: Cameron 'Buck' Williams, like the central character in *666*, is a journalist who witnesses the rapture while travelling on a plane; like Tom Hammond, from Watson's earlier series, he is a thirty-year old bachelor who is given the opportunity to launch his own news source. Other stock characters include Bruce Barnes, as the pastor who lacked real faith and was consequently left behind.

But *Left Behind* is as much about politics as biblical exegesis. A growing suspicion of 'old Europe' is echoed in the fact that the rising Antichrist – Nicolae Carpathia – is a Romanian who hijacks the ambitions of the U.N. In the threat they represent, conspiring Eastern Europeans are the new Jews sucking the blood of western democracy (before *Left Behind*, Bram Stoker's Dracula was literature's most famous Carpathian, and Nicolae Ceausescu was the last Communist dictator of Romania). Readers will be similarly unsurprised by the basic shape of the plot, which clearly echoes the foundational patterns of the genre. The novels take no pains to conceal this borrowing – *Assassins* (1999) is dedicated to John F. Walvoord, one of the most famous representatives of classical dispensationalism, whose life-long commitment to the movement 'has helped keep the torch of prophecy burning'. As the dedication suggests, the novels endorse a particular variant of dispensationalism while combining rapture fiction's standard themes with contemporary political and cultural concerns.[42]

But it would be unfair to dismiss the series as entirely derivative. There are some surprising differences with the rapture fiction tradition. It is important to note, for example, that the rapture imagined by Jenkins and LaHaye is quite different from that represented in mainstream dispensationalism. Earlier writers, not taking at face value the opinion poll calculations of those Americans claiming to be 'born again', would have regarded the huge numbers of those involved in *Left Behind*'s rapture as hopelessly optimistic: more than one hundred passengers on Rayford's 747 are among the disappeared.[43] But the percentage increases. In *Apocalypse Dawn* (2003), a spin-off from the original *Left Behind* project, which is marketed under its franchise, the rapture removes 'a third of the world's population'.[44] This vast number is given a geographical break-down:

> Africa and South America had been hardest hit, with Europe next in line, and the Middle and Far East hardly touched ... In some places in the United States, the equivalent of whole towns had vanished ... China might have lost ten million.[45]

Equally innovative is the rapture's inclusion of the unborn and all pre-teenage children, demonstrating the impact of anti-abortion rhetoric on the increasingly politicised American evangelical community. But perhaps the most significant aspect of *Left Behind*'s rapture is that it includes the Pope.

The novels' presentation of Catholicism has often been criticised, but observers have consistently failed to appreciate the watershed in evangelical opinion that these novels represent. Historically, evangelical exegetes have either identified the Pope as the Antichrist or have predicted that Roman Catholicism would be central in the end-times persecution of true believers. *Left Behind* challenges these assumptions, echoing a major re-thinking of evangelical attitudes to Catholicism and the hugely influential rapprochement represented by the project of Charles Colson and R. J. Neuhaus's *Evangelicals and Catholics Together: The Christian Mission in the Third Millennium* (1994). The novels seem to want to have their cake and eat it. In one novel, an entire congregation of Catholics is represented as among the 'raptured', with no hint or suggestion that they were closet evangelicals.[46] The situation is more ambivalent with the raptured Pope, John XXIV, who is included in the rapture perhaps because he has been criticised by Catholic theologians for his interest in promoting Lutheran reform.[47] His name and interests invite comparison with the reforming and ecumenical interests of Pope John XXIII (1958-63), who called the Second Vatican Council and received Geoffrey Fisher on the first visit of an Archbishop of Canterbury to the Vatican.[48] Despite this attempt at conciliation, however, the novels simultaneously endorse the traditional evangelical reading of the Vatican's role in the prophetic future. John XXIV's replacement is identified as the eschatological 'false prophet', and the new one-world religion that Antichrist sponsors is centred, initially, on the Vatican.[49]

The series' references to demonic one-world systems illustrate the extent to which the novels reinforce the standard themes of political fear exploited by the American prophetic tradition. In the aftermath of the Cold War, the novels reinvent dispensational pessimism by representing the effect of the meltdown of the superpowers.[50] The well-being of established nation states is contrasted with the political ambition of the U.N., which, in response to the global catastrophe of the rapture, begins to build the one-world government that dispensational exponents have historically feared. Combining administrative prowess with entrepreneurial wizardry, the U.N. oversees the introduction of a single world currency, taking a 0.1% tax on every dollar spent.[51] The administrative infrastructure required to make this possible is the stuff of urban legends. The novels reach into the world of their readers when they refer to a supercomputer called 'the Beast'; since 1983, evangelical prophecy 'experts' have repeatedly claimed that a machine with this name actually exists at the heart of the European administration in Brussels.[52] Similar appeals to current prophetic speculation lend weight to the novels' claim that bar code and bio-chip technology make possible the electronic 'mark of the beast'.[53] The novels put a spin on contemporary advances in veterinary science by tracing Antichrist's ability to implant the electronic mark into humans to the existing method of injecting electronic tags into pets.[54] With technology thereby providing the means of electronic commerce and population control, the foundations are laid for Antichrist's centralised bureaucracy: 'one economy highlighted by one currency, no need for passports, one government, eventually one language, one system of measurement, and one religion.'[55] The new world government is the dream of the European Union writ large: 'Today is the first day of the rest of utopia.'[56]

But one man's millennium is another man's tribulation. With his control of the population largely established, Carpathia wages his own 'culture war', aiming to overturn traditional taste by targeting the classical and the beautiful, destroying valued art treasures, and seizing control of crucial media.[57] Antichrist, in other words, will consolidate the existing marginalisation of the American evangelical community. With broadcasting and publishing in his power, only the internet is free from his spin.[58] This control of minds is linked to his attempt to control bodies; his ethical policies, peppered with the demands of contemporary liberals, descend to the fascist, idealising 'proper legislation concerning abortion, assisted suicide, and the reduction of expensive care for the defective and handicapped'.[59] Neither does 'the most technologically advanced regime in history' accommodate dissent.[60] Carpathia's administration creates 'the most powerful enforcement juggernaut the world has ever seen'.[61] In the face of this hegemony, the series' evangelicals epitomise American individualism as they mobilise to resist: 'the very idea of a one-world government, or currency, or especially faith … is from the pit of hell.'[62]

Their resistance is significant, in that it negotiates the problematic silence of the prophetic Scriptures: what happens to America? The novels affirm the dispensational tradition that the USA has no role in biblical prophecy and that, they conclude, must mean that America is largely destroyed.[63] The means by which this is achieved are startling to anyone who reads these novels as an expression of contemporary evangelical opinion, for America fails when the world needs it most. Opposition to the U.N.'s new one-world regime comes, significantly, from the American President, Gerald Fitzhugh, described as 'a younger version of Lyndon Johnson' and 'the greatest friend Israel ever had'.[64] But the president is out of step with his military. When his top brass promise support for Carpathia's programme, the president finds his only allies in the right-wing militias.[65] These 'patriotic militia forces' are 'surprisingly organised', the novels note, but despite their support by Egypt and 'England' (rather than the UK), their military resistance is futile.[66] British and American cities are destroyed in a brief nuclear war.[67]

Resistance is therefore focused on the surviving evangelical communities – the self-styled and neo-survivalist 'Tribulation

Force'. The novels' description of social norms among these post-rapture evangelicals is fascinating. Conversion and church fellowship are alike figured with tactility: Buck, who 'had already fallen in love with God,' noted lots of hugging, 'especially among men'.[68] As in other examples of the genre, scenes in the local fellowship are the means of disseminating dispensationalism's central hermeneutic:

> Rayford was more than fascinated. ... Not long ago he would have scoffed at such teaching, at such a literal take on so clearly a poetic and metaphorical passage. But what Bruce said made sense.[69]

Simultaneously, these discussions of the 'literal hermeneutic' – now confirmed by recent fulfilments of erstwhile expectations – defend the assumptions of the novels' implied audience against contemporary derision that 'right-wing, fanatical, fundamentalist factions ... have always taken the Bible literally'.[70] So, the novels argue, does God.

Nevertheless, the narratives do take unexpected turns, and the tribulation offers unexpected opportunities. When secure communication is possible only through the internet, Chloe begins her resistance to Antichrist's global power by establishing an alternative economy, based on resistance to the 'mark of the beast', by developing an international Co-op.[71] Building a worldwide business empire is a peculiarly American method of combating the tyranny and evil of the Antichrist. Her Tribulation Force partner, Tsion Ben-Judah, likewise disseminates his prophetic teaching through 'the most popular Web site in history'.[72] The regime bans all access to the site, but their attempt at regulation proves impossible to monitor, and Tsion's 'Internet church' explodes in its numbers of adherents.[73] Faith, technology and entrepreneurialism are the new faith, hope and love.

AFTER LEFT BEHIND

But the innovations continue in the aftermath of *Left Behind*. The success of the first batch of novels has led the project's managers to market an additional four new series based on the original themes. LaHaye's defence of the expanding project has harked back to Watson's pragmatic defence of his earlier rapture fictions: 'The fantastic popularity of the Left Behind series ... convinced me that fiction is a powerful way for me to share with readers some of what I find so completely fascinating about end times prophecies.'[74] Thus, while LaHaye and Jenkins have continued to work on prequels and a sequel to the original twelve-volume series, they have independently developed new ideas. Some of these new projects have developed earlier themes in unanticipated ways.

LaHaye teamed up with Greg Dinallo to publish *Babylon Rising* (2004), moving out of the world of evangelical publishing to work with Bantam Dell, a division of Random House. *Babylon Rising* is the first instalment of a new series that centres on an evangelical version of Indiana Jones, 'an unlikely academic' who lectures in archaeology at a North Carolina university.[75] In the novel, Professor Michael Murphy sets out on a quest to search for the missing pieces of the bronze serpent, made by Moses, destroyed by Hezekiah, but, apparently, preserved by a secret cult for the last days, when its recovery will herald the rising again of 'the dark power of Babylon'.[76] His discoveries lead him into another search for the remnants of the Nebuchadnezzar's statue (Daniel 2:31-45), with all its significance as an indicator of the fate of world empires.

Like previous rapture fictions, *Babylon Rising* uses its material to defend a conservative evangelical worldview. This defence is made possible by the novel's description of Murphy's introductory lecture, for example, which refers to 'more than *thirty thousand* different archaeological digs that have unearthed evidence supporting the Old Testament'.[77] The novel reiterates the familiar claim that 'prophecy ... is history written in advance', and argues that 'there are more Biblical reasons to believe that Christ will return to set up His kingdom in our lifetime than in any generation before us'.[78] But the novel also develops political and cultural fears when it imagines that 'Babylon will rise a second time and rule the entire world'.[79] As in earlier novels, the United Nations is a threat to American peace:

> We don't believe the U.N. is evil … We believe it does some good work. Peacekeeping in certain third world countries where there is chaos, humanitarian aid, health programs, and so on. But we are suspicious about their efforts to promote globalism by uniting all religions regardless of their beliefs, and by uniting the world's governments under a single entity. In particular, I'm very concerned about turning the sovereignty of the United States government over to a world court.[80]

The concern is closely related to the statue in Daniel: 'Prophecy experts believe the toes – made of clay and iron – represent an unstable form of government that will take over from today's nation states in the near future. Probably ten kings or rulers of some kind, paving the way for the Antichrist.'[81] But this kind of opposition to the U.N. is misunderstood, and the novel focuses on the sense of the marginalisation of believers that so often marks the post-*Left Behind* novels. Powerful forces, working to undermine the good character of American evangelicals, portray them as 'dangerous fanatics'.[82] The FBI holds files on 'fringe Christian groups that are ranting and raving about the U.N.'[83] Believers with end-times interests are regarded as a 'vast conspiracy' in a 'smear campaign' that claims the existence of 'a basement bomb factory run by evangelical Christian extremists'.[84]

With its big-name publisher and marketing panache, *Babylon Rising* emphasised LaHaye's role in the success of *Left Behind*. The cover of the British edition referred to him as 'the world's best-selling supernatural thriller author', and LaHaye's various dedications inside the novel included thanks to 'Jerry B. Jenkins, my co-author and partner in the Left Behind series, which has turned into a publishing phenomenon, who worked with me to bring to the printed page my vision of a fictional portrayal of Bible prophecy'.[85] After the dedications, *Babylon Rising* presented 'A Message from Tim LaHaye', which welcomed first-time readers of 'my fiction writing' to 'my new prophetic fiction series', though it referred to Jenkins as a co-author of the earlier material. More recently, LaHaye has again switched writing partners. In the new series' most recent instalment, *The Secret on Ararat* (2004), Greg Dinallo has been replaced by Bob Phillips.

Jerry B. Jenkins' new prophecy series has also focused on the period before the rapture, but imagines that the rapture will be postponed by at least forty years and that a future America will be a totalitarian state committed to the wholesale persecution of believers. In *Soon* (2003), this persecution takes believers back to their New Testament situation, when Christians were also 'persona non grata with the government and had to meet in secret and worship virtually underground.'[86] This opportunity for a new beginning allows the believers to dispense with the traditional markers of denominational adherence. As we will see, in describing a world where Christians can do without the ordinances of the church, *Soon* reflects the ecclesiastical weakness of a great deal of contemporary evangelicalism. But it also reflects a changing world situation. We have already noticed that the end of the Cold War challenged many of these novels' assumptions, and demanded that the rapture be re-written. *Left Behind* made a valiant attempt to address the end of communism. *Soon* develops the trend by abandoning the East-West division that so many earlier rapture fictions had presupposed, choosing to situate the struggle between good and evil within America itself. The radical restructuring of dispensationalism that began in *Left Behind* has been significantly developed in *Soon*; for America, it argues, has begun to change.[87]

Yet *Soon* suggests that evangelicalism has also begun to change. Ironically, this new evangelicalism grows in its capacity for violence as it loses its theological edge. In *Left Behind*, Rayford had prayed for the 'privilege' of torturing and killing the Antichrist, even though he knew that his death would only make him stronger after his resurrection.[88] Tsion Ben-Judah had also defended the right of the believer to use violence on his enemies: 'I believe we are at war. In the heat of battle, killing the enemy has never been considered murder.'[89] In the context of 9-11, it is hardly surprising that the Antichrist's advisors wonder whether Rayford believes he is fighting a 'holy war': 'Then I guess anything goes.'[90] It takes a long time – and several novels – for Rayford to come to terms with the fact that he has to love his enemies: 'We don't play them, lie to them, cheat them, steal from them, blackmail them. We love them. We plead with them.'[91] Even in the tribulation, evangelicals have to love their enemies and try to win them to Christ.

Soon underplays this responsibility. Some of the novel's characters remember the violence of Christian fundamentalists during the first decade of the new millennium:

> religious extremists ... persecuted homosexuals, assassinated abortion doctors ... and bombed stem-cell research labs ... And after the terrorist attacks of '05, it was the extremists who defied the tolerance laws and rioted, killing Muslims.[92]

But if this violence had generated state oppression, the believers appear not to have learned the lesson. Their capacity for violence is displayed in the Watchmen, the novel's equivalent of *Left Behind*'s Tribulation Force. The Watchmen are organising 'Operation Soon', an evangelism project designed to spread the (illegal) news that the 'terrorist attacks' the government is resisting are actually miracles that should be understood as signs of the second coming. To survive the persecution, the Watchmen build a massive underground complex in an abandoned mine, and safeguard their privacy by posting armed guards. The guards are prepared to kill intruders, returning the corpse to the surface, 'putting it in the vehicle it showed up in, and moving that vehicle somewhere so the body would not be traced to the mine'.[93] Paul Stepola, the novel's principal character, was shocked by the revelation:

> 'How do you justify that?'
> 'We don't, Paul. We pray it never happens.'[94]

With attitudes like these, it is no wonder that the government can dismiss the disturbing supernatural events as illegal actions in a 'Christian Guerrilla War'.[95]

Another first instalment of a new series – Mel Odom's *Apocalypse Dawn* (2003) – is equally concerning. While the novel is perhaps better written than the first series, it is also much less careful in its theological statements. *Apocalypse Dawn* shares the *Left Behind* branding and is marketed by the earlier series' evangelical publishers. It self-consciously maps onto the plot structure of *Left Behind*. Significant characters appear in both sets of narratives, for example, and the new series clearly borrows the earlier prophetic timetable. Significantly, however, *Apocalypse Dawn* re-writes the terms of those who would be involved in the rapture. In the new series, the mere possession of faith is no longer enough to guarantee that the tribulation will be escaped. Delroy, a Navy chaplain, missed the rapture. Years earlier, he had 'found the Lord', but he 'didn't stay walking close to the Lord'.[96] He states that he was left behind because he was only 'a *pretty good* Christian … I didn't believe with the strength and the faith and the conviction I was supposed to.'[97] In prayer, Delroy concludes, 'I know you left me behind because I have broken the relationship I have had with You. Is this my punishment then, God, for doubting You?'[98]

These statements revolutionise the rapture. Either *Apocalypse Dawn* is describing a partial rapture, in which only the holiest believers are taken, or it is assuming, like *Left Behind*, that the rapture included all of the saved, but that Delroy had (temporarily) lost his salvation. Neither of these approaches would please the majority of mainstream dispensationalists – nor would they satisfy the criteria of biblical truth. But the confusion continues. Odom's book consistently assumes that we are saved by the amount of our faith, rather than by the object of our faith. In other words, faith has to reach a certain level before it guarantees salvation. Throughout *Apocalypse Dawn*, those characters that move towards saving faith are depicted as re-activating a faith they had allowed to grow dim. The tragedy of being left behind is simply explained: 'We didn't believe enough.'[99] Those who are left behind are 'the non-believers … And those who only gave belief lip service. And those … who had doubts.'[100] The *Left Behind* franchise is moving far beyond orthodoxy.

These statements engage in pastoral cruelty. No Christian ever has enough faith, and the Christian's doubts are real. But these doubts do not preclude our salvation. Psalm 88 offers strange statements for the language of faith, but there is no suggestion in this psalm, one of several psalms that do not end in hope, that its statements are inappropriate for the life of the believer.[101] Nor is our salvation something that we can have and lose. After all, even when the psalmist fears that God has 'cast off' his soul (Ps. 88:14), he is still able to refer to him as the 'God of my salvation' (v. 1). Yet, throughout *Apocalypse Dawn*, the emphasis is consistently on faith's strength, rather than on faith's object: 'How strong did faith have to be?'[102] Only as strong or as large as a mustard seed, Jesus taught (Matt. 17:20); what is important is not the degree of faith, but whether faith is placed in him.

CONCLUSION

Tragically, this basic theological confusion goes hand-in-hand with commercial success and evangelical celebration. As the internet and business success of Tsion and Chloe illustrates, fortunes and reputations can be made in the tribulation – and not only by characters in the series. In *Left Behind*, Jenkins and LaHaye tend to limit their plot to the seven years of tribulation. The first ten of the series' twelve novels, for example, contain only a handful of references to the future thousand-year reign of Christ.[103] This concentration on apocalyptic rather than millennial themes is justified by a claim that more Scripture is devoted to the last three and a half years of the tribulation than to 'any other period except the life of Christ'.[104] But there can be little doubt that market forces also find it more congenial. Disaster fictions always sell, and the reason they sell to evangelicals is because these kinds of fictions emerge as the movement anticipates a future of acute crisis. Another reason why they sell is that evangelicals have lost the capacity to judge whether the novels' theological presuppositions are actually true. 'Nothing could have been scripted like this', thought Buck, but he, as a writer, should have known.[105] The history of rapture fiction demonstrates that it's not easy to say something new about the end of the world – and proves that evangelicals will buy almost anything.

Chapter 4

LEFT BEHIND AND THE GOSPEL

"Pastor Billings walked the viewers of that tape through a prayer. We were to tell God we knew we were sinners and that we needed his forgiveness. We were to tell him we believed Jesus died for our sins and God raised him from the dead. Then we were to accept his gift of salvation and thank him for it."

"Seems too easy."[1]

And, perhaps, it is. Within the culture of evangelicalism, there is no more serious charge than to suggest that any Christian speaker or writer has misrepresented the gospel. It should never be done lightly, for, as Paul argues in Galatians 1, the stakes are incredibly high. Yet it is the claim of this book that rapture fictions have often emerged from an unhealthy evangelicalism; that they often represent a faith that is significantly different from that defended by earlier dispensationalists; and, far more importantly, that they often represent a faith that is different from that outlined in Scripture. Fundamentally, this chapter argues, something should not be uncritically accepted simply because it wears the 'evangelical' label and has generated wide success. The motto of the Christian reader should always be 'Prove all things; hold fast that which is good' (1 Thess. 5:21).

There can be no doubt that *Left Behind*, like other rapture fictions, has deliberately aimed at 'that which is good'. At the beginning of the twentieth century, Sydney Watson made his books' evangelistic purpose clear, claiming that 'many thousands have read, and have been awakened, quickened, even converted' by *Scarlet and Purple* (1913) and other Christian novels.[2] Watson defended his novels on that pragmatic basis – how could it be wrong to turn theology into fiction, if God was so clearly using his books to win souls?

Before the publication of *Left Behind*, Tim LaHaye and Jerry B. Jenkins had demonstrated their commitment to communicating their understanding of the gospel. Jenkins has had a long career as a writer and editor of biblically-conservative publications, while LaHaye has been a long-standing advocate of traditional family values.[3] Both men had published best-sellers long before they began work on the *Left Behind* project. Jenkins has published over 150 books, including ghost-written biographies of several sports stars and evangelical leaders, and had worked on Billy Graham's best-selling biography, *Just as I am* (1997). LaHaye had been a pastor and political leader, and had published over 50 books, among which his titles on marriage and temperament change had generated huge successes. No one who had looked at their busy workloads and considerable output could have doubted that these authors had been using their respected gifts to advance the cause of Jesus Christ. But their several rapture fictions have been far more successful than the Watson trilogy, and, unlike Watson, they have pointed to specific instances in which God has apparently used their novels for the conversion of others. Their writing is clearly persuasive. No one could read their novels without realising that they have been written to change minds and, ultimately, to change lives.

And there is evidence that Jenkins and LaHaye have been enabled to achieve these goals. The fourth book in the *Left Behind* series, *Soul Harvest* (1998), was dedicated to 'our brand-new brothers and sisters' – evidently those who had made a profession of faith after reading novels in the series. At the end of 2002, *Today's Christian* reported that the authors had received letters from 3,000 people indicating that they had 'received Christ' after reading the *Left Behind* books.[4] In 2003, the authors teamed up with biographer Norman B. Rohrer to illustrate the series' life-changing potential. *These Will Not Be Left Behind: True Stories of Changed Lives* documented a number of testimonies of those whose profession of faith had been directly linked to the books.

So, it could be argued, if God is blessing this series, it would be churlish and judgemental to be concerned about its presentation of the Christian faith. But across the evangelical board, other writers have expressed concern at the series' representation of the gospel.[5] Is it possible that *Left Behind* contains a serious misrepresentation of the Christian faith?[6]

WHERE LEFT BEHIND IS RIGHT

Left Behind often gets it right. In fact, there is no doubt that many of the criticisms directed at the series could be directed, with equal justification, at evangelicalism in general. The series' moral commitments, for example, reflect its authors' conservative American situation but do also tend to emerge from a basic evangelical adherence to Scripture. While the Bible may not advocate suspicion of all political leaders emerging at a young age from Eastern Europe, its discussion of the sanctity of human life would certainly insist on the wrongs of Carpathia's policies on abortion and euthanasia. And there is no attempt to map a distinctive evangelical faith onto the American population at large. While Jenkins and LaHaye write with a much-criticised combination of American patriotism and evangelical hope, they are nevertheless painfully aware of the minority status of their faith. At times, the novels are only too aware of the chasm between the evangelical faith and American popular religion:

> Had you asked people on the street five minutes before the Rapture what Christians taught about God and heaven, nine in ten would have told you that the church expected them to lead a good life, to do the best they could, to think of others, to be kind, to live in peace. It sounded so good, and yet it was so wrong.[7]

Not everything about the series deserves condemnation, therefore, nor should evangelicals distance themselves from all of the criticisms directed at the series. *Left Behind* is not complacent about the spiritual state of America.

How appropriate, therefore, that the novels emphasise the importance of the gospel. The series first exemplifies the movement from popular American religiosity to genuine faith when Irene Steele, wife of one of the series' most significant characters, becomes interested in 'real preaching and teaching'.[8] Much to her husband's consternation, she becomes preoccupied 'with the end of the world, with the love of Jesus, with the salvation of souls'.[9] Rayford is not altogether happy with the changes in his wife, and finds her new church just 'a little too literal and personal and challenging'.[10] *Left Behind* presents the journey towards true faith as a journey towards the social margins.

While the success of their series has catapulted dispensational ideas into the centre of American popular culture, therefore, the authors are only too aware of the marginal status of their convictions. Despite recent conservative victories, the novels imply, Americans cannot assume that the patriotic rhetoric of the state shares any vital dynamic of saving faith. Yet, at the same time, the series is incredibly optimistic about the number of people who will be involved in the rapture. On Rayford's flight, 'more than a hundred people' are among the disappeared.[11] In Mel Odom's *Apocalypse Dawn* and Nessa Hart's *End of State* (2003), both marketed by the original publisher as part of the *Left Behind* franchise, one third of the global population disappears.[12]

While these figures look incredibly optimistic, neither Jenkins nor LaHaye could be accused of complacency about the human condition. Pausing from fast-paced action, one character in *Desecration* explains that humanity is 'born in sin and separated from God'.[13] *Nicolae* explains that good works cannot purchase salvation because

> the Bible is clear that all our righteousnesses are like filthy rags. There is none righteous, no not one. We have turned, every one, to his own way. All have sinned and fall short of the glory of God. In the economy of God, we are all worthy only of the punishment of death.[14]

Salvation, the novels properly continue, 'is the gift of God, not of works, lest anyone should boast'.[15]

Theologically, the novels are at their best when, as here, they simply echo Scripture. These quotations, for example, pull together statements from Isaiah 64:6, Romans 3:10, Isaiah 53:6 and Romans 3:23 to accurately reflect a number of central themes in the biblical teaching of human need. The novels exhort their readers to 'understand the depth of your own depravity' and to realise that those who are not Christians are 'dead in … sins'.[16] As one character puts it, 'you need to be saved because you cannot save yourself.'[17] The novels are equally insistent that salvation can only come through Jesus Christ. He is the one who 'offers the free gift of salvation to anyone who believes'.[18] His kingdom is 'exclusively for those who have made the right decision … [to] call on the name of the Lord'.[19] *Left Behind* often gets it wonderfully right.

WHERE LEFT BEHIND IS WRONG

But, problematically, *Left Behind* often also gets it wrong. The series mirrors both the strengths and weaknesses of the evangelical world from which it emerges, and demonstrates the extent to which the movement has been influenced by the tactile romanticism of the age. Buck describes his conversion as his having 'fallen in love with God', for example, and, new to congregational worship, marvels at 'all this hugging, especially among men'.[20] For many readers, this will not be strange. The difficulty for these readers will be to distinguish the spirit of the gospel from the spirit of the age, to see where American or popular evangelical values end and where biblical principles actually begin.

This undifferentiated combination of American evangelical values and biblical principles is evident in the series' identification of a group of people who do not need to be saved. Unlike some earlier rapture fictions, *Left Behind* includes among the disappeared both unborn babies and pre-teenage children. Undoubtedly this reflects the growing politicisation of the American Christian right. Tim LaHaye has been an outspoken defender of family values, and has organised anti-abortion campaigns to defend the 'right to life'. Throughout history, evangelicals have always debated the fate of those who died in infancy or in the womb. In *Left Behind*, these hopes are defined in a theology of the 'age of accountability'. In a video he had prepared for those who would be left behind, Pastor Billings explained the sudden disappearance of children and unborn babies:

> Up to a certain age, which is probably different for each individual, we believe God will not hold a child accountable for a decision that must be made with heart and mind, fully cognizant of the ramifications.[21]

In its most basic form, this idea signals that those who die before they are able to understand the gospel will not be held accountable for their sins. In Odom's *Apocalypse Dawn*, that age is specified – every child 'from newborn to the age of twelve'[22] is among the disappeared.

There is some biblical support for this idea. David, for example, had high hopes for his son when he died at birth, and expected to see him in the future life (2 Sam. 12:23). But it would be a mistake to imagine that children and the unborn can be guaranteed salvation without experiencing the gracious activity of God. Individuals are not only condemned for their own misdeeds, but also for the original sin they inherit from Adam. The death of the unborn can be explained on no other basis: their death is 'the wages of sin' (Rom. 6:23), for 'death passed upon all men, for that all have sinned' (Rom. 5:12). The unborn are not too young to know the effect of sin, but neither are they too young to know the effect of grace: John the Baptist was filled with the Holy Spirit within his mother's womb (Luke 1:15). Nevertheless, the 'age of accountability' doctrine is an attempt to weave a pattern of belief that one cannot exegete from Scripture. It would be a mistake to assume that anyone is too young to know the grace of God, or to imagine that heaven can be gained without the application of salvation. When the implications of the fall are taken into account, there is no such thing as an innocent child. If all children under the age of twelve are saved, they are saved because God has applied to them the benefits of his Son's death.

The series' combination of American evangelical values and biblical principles is equally apparent in its presentation of the gospel. The novels balance the limited number of the saved with the claim that those who are not among their number have only themselves to blame. Countering the notion that the evangelical gospel is 'exclusivistic', one character exhorts his listener to 'Understand this: The Bible makes it clear that the will of God is that all men be saved.'[23] The novels accurately reflect the Bible's insistence on the universality of the gospel: 'He is the one who offers the free gift of salvation to anyone who believes!'[24] At the same time, problematically, they base that free offer on an unqualified portrayal of God's ineffective longing to bring salvation to all humanity. Quoting 2 Peter 3:9, one character reminds the readers that 'God is not willing that any should perish but that all should come to repentance.'[25] But there is no explanation as to why the God who predicts and controls the history of the world cannot influence the personal history of its individuals. If, in the novels, he wants to pour judgements on the earth, he can do so; but we are never told why he cannot save every individual, if, as the citation of 2 Peter 3:9 appears to suggest, that is exactly what he wants.

The picture the novels present is of a waiting and hopeful God, who has issued a general invitation to salvation but leaves individuals free to decide on their own destiny. The novels claim that 'we have an august God – the only supreme, omnipotent potentate.'[26] But, they continue,

> if the Bible teaches us one thing about God, it is that he is for us. He is not against us. He wants to bless our lives, and the key to the door of blessing is to give your life to him and ask him to do with it as he will.[27]

Effectively, therefore, the series does not represent God as sovereign. This 'supreme, omnipotent' king stands idly by while humanity decides whether or not to use the key to the 'door of blessing'. God's omnipotence does not ordinarily extend into the lives of individuals, neither the often confusing events of world history, nor the clouds in the sky. In fact, all things considered, he is not really worthy of being called 'omnipotent' at all:

> For generations people have called natural disasters "acts of God." This has been a misnomer. Eons ago, God the Father conceded control of Earth's weather to Satan himself, the prince and power of the air. ... And no doubt God at times intervened against such actions by the evil one because of the fervent prayers of his people.[28]

'Conceded' is an extremely significant term in any discussion of God's sovereignty – not least when Scripture represents God as actively engaged in controlling the weather (Job 38:22-29). Nevertheless, the novels rather frankly admit, 'God left control of [the world] pretty much to Satan.'[29] It seems, in the theology of *Left Behind*, that God is a careless absentee monarch who has devolved responsibility for his world to a powerful and vindictive enemy.

This undermining of divine sovereignty makes the series' presentation of the gospel extremely problematic. If, as the novels claim, Satan is 'pretty much' in control of the world, apparently able to limit God's access to its environment, and if, as Scripture and the novels agree, individuals are 'dead in trespasses and sins', it is difficult to see how anyone could be saved at all. The novels suggest that God has no ability to intervene in anyone's state of spiritual death. But if the novels present a faulty view of God, their representation of salvation is equally concerning.

LEFT BEHIND AND THE 'SINNER'S PRAYER'

Left Behind, like rapture fictions more generally, does not have much theological coherence beyond its well-known dispensationalism. The question of the sinner's ability to respond to the gospel is never seriously addressed. Describing the sinner's 'depravity', and showing him to be 'dead in trespasses and sins', the series elaborates a theological conundrum that shows characters coming to faith in Christ despite the opposition of the persecuting world, the almost-all-controlling devil, and the revolution of the flesh. The meaning of spiritual death is never fully considered in the series. If 'there is none that seeketh after God' (Rom. 3:11), and God cannot seek after individuals, then there is no basis for their reconciliation. If individuals are 'dead' to God, and he is unable to press his attentions upon them, it is impossible that anyone should be saved. But, in the novels, reconciliation is possible, and frequently attained, through characters' use of the 'Sinner's Prayer'.

Throughout the series, repenting sinners are repeatedly exhorted to use the Sinner's Prayer – a prayer which, once recited, is expected to guarantee salvation. It is variously stated, but always returns to the same handful of themes:

> The God who created you loves you. His Son who died for your sins will return ... How do you receive Christ? Merely tell God that you know you are a sinner and that you need him. Accept the gift of salvation, believe that Christ is risen, and say so.[30]

> God, I know I'm a sinner ... Forgive my sins and come into my life and save me ... Thank you for sending your Son to die on the cross for me ... I accept your gift and receive you right now ... Amen.[31]

Dear God, I am a sinner and separated from you. I believe
Jesus is the Messiah and that he died on the cross to pay
for my sins. I believe that he rose again the third day and
that by receiving his gift of love I will have the power
to become a son of God because I believe on his name.
Thank you for hearing me and saving me, and I pledge
the rest of my life to you.[32]

Tell God that you acknowledge that you are a sinner and
are separated from him. Tell him you know that nothing
you can do for yourself will earn your way to him. Tell
him you believe that he sent his Son, Jesus Christ, to die
on the cross for your sins, that he was raised from the
dead, has raptured his church, and is coming yet again
to the earth. Receive him as your Savior right where you
are.[33]

With this repeated emphasis, the novels' debt to twentieth-
century evangelicalism is clear. The efficacy of the Sinner's Prayer
is one of the most cherished myths in contemporary evangelical
church life. Advocates of its merit have included many of the most
famous evangelists of the twentieth century. The Sinner's Prayer
can find support from many of the most significant leaders across
the evangelical world.

But that does not mean that it is right. Christians are commanded to 'prove all things', and when we do, we discover that the
method of salvation that commonly surrounds the Sinner's Prayer
is almost entirely a twentieth-century phenomenon. This staple
element of modern evangelical conversion did not exist for most
of the history of the church. Far more seriously, the methodol-
ogy of the Sinner's Prayer is entirely without biblical foundation.
Across the world, evangelical churches are filled with people who
believe that they are Christians on the basis of a prayer they once
prayed. But the Bible never teaches us that we are saved through
a prayer. Neither do the apostles ever instruct their hearers that
praying a prayer with these specified components will guarantee
salvation. This emphasis on the Sinner's Prayer is perhaps one of

the most concerning aspects of the novels' presentation of the gospel, for we are saved by faith, not the utterance of a prayer, and it is only too possible that the mechanistic idea of salvation the novels develop will encourage people without saving faith to believe they have been saved because they have recited a set form of words. The Sinner's Prayer is a myth that has made possible the corruption of the modern evangelical church, channelling many who have never known the saving grace of God into membership of his churches. It provides its own word of assurance: 'Thank you for hearing me and saving me, and I pledge the rest of my life to you.'[34] Tragically, it convinces people that they are Christians when too often they are not.

Rayford faced this problem of assurance while witnessing to Mac in *Soul Harvest* (1998). He explained that Christ's death covered 'everybody's sin' and that 'all we had to do was believe that, repent of our sins, receive the gift of salvation':

> "I believe all that, Ray, so is that it? Am I in?"
> Rayford's blood ran cold. ... This was too easy.[35]

And indeed it is too easy. The Sinner's Prayer provides an unstable and uncertain foundation for assurance, and raises more difficulties than it solves. Mac's apparent coolness to the meaning of the prayer dramatises a fear that stalks the evangelical imagination and drives many to frequent repetitions of its terms. Far from providing true assurance, it often completely undermines it.

The great danger of this traditional evangelical method is that the prayer of faith becomes the object of faith, and the Sinner's Prayer becomes the sinner's hope. In spiritual crises, the anxious soul looks back to words that were prayed, and the assurance these words were believed to guarantee. Yet these words cannot bring salvation – only faith can do that. Our words cannot generate assurance – that springs from the secret working of the Holy Spirit, sowing in believers the graces that John describes in his first epistle. There is false assurance as well as true – note Jesus' insistence that 'those Jews which believed on him' were actually 'of [their] father the devil' (John 8:31, 44). A great danger of these novels is that their focus on the Sinner's Prayer points the uncertain to an uncertain basis for hope.

In other words, *Left Behind* significantly rewrites the apostolic presentation of the gospel. New Testament preachers never exhorted their listeners to repent on the basis of the imminent second coming; in rapture fictions that is a reiterated appeal. Similarly, for reasons that will later become obvious, most rapture fictions do not expect their characters' conversions to follow the pattern established in the New Testament church. Instead of leading their repentant listeners through a prayer, the apostles exhorted them to faith and repentance and insisted their conversion be immediately sealed in baptism and church fellowship: 'Sirs, what must I do to be saved? And they said, Believe on the Lord Jesus Christ, and thou shalt be saved, and thy house' (Acts 16:30-31). The great danger of the novels' presentation of the gospel is that many of their readers could pray the Sinner's Prayer, and with no teaching on assurance, imagine that that believing they are saved is the same as actually being saved.

In *Babylon Rising* (2004), Tim LaHaye provides something of a theological improvement on the earlier series. The novel's hero, Michael Murphy, discussed the nature of God with sheikh Umar al-Khaliq:

> "According to the Bible, a person becomes a Christian by believing that Jesus Christ is not only the Son of God who died for the sins of the world, but that He rose again on the third day and will save all who call on Him by faith."
>
> "That is all? It seems too easy, too simple."
>
> Murphy nodded. "Yes, it does. … In the quiet of your own thoughts you can call out to the Father in the name of the Son, and the Holy Spirit will save you and give you eternal life."[36]

The sheikh is a minor character who returns at the end of the novel as a convert to Christianity, but his conversion seems to have a firmer grounding than many of those presented in the earlier series.[37]

FREE WILL AND THE SECOND CHANCE

Many supporters and critics of dispensationalism might be surprised to learn that *Left Behind*'s presentation of the gospel is a long way from that preferred by J. N. Darby – perhaps nowhere more obviously than in the novels' representation of human freedom. In 1861, Darby wrote a letter lamenting 'this fresh breaking out of the doctrine of free will'. 'All men who have never been deeply convinced of sin … believe more or less in free will', he complained, despite the fact that it 'completely changes all the idea of Christianity and entirely perverts it.'[38] Darby believed that freedom of the will had been lost at the fall, and unsaved humanity was now bound over to wickedness. In that state, 'to leave [an unbeliever] to his own choice, now that he is disposed to do evil, would be a cruelty'.[39] Instead, the will had to be changed by God, so that the individual would be enabled to repent and believe (Ephesians 2:8; Acts 11:18). In contrast, modern rapture novels develop a theology of free will that assumes its centrality in evangelism while anticipating its gradual weakening throughout the tribulation.

This theology of free will emerges from the *Left Behind* series' concept of the 'second chance'. The novels encourage those of their readers who have not prayed the Sinner's Prayer to believe that they will have another opportunity for salvation after the rapture. The point is made clear in *Apocalypse Dawn*: 'All those who have not come to know Jesus Christ as their Saviour before the Rapture will be given one last chance to make their peace with him and their acceptance of his dominion over their lives.'[40] Second chance theology – the idea that those who had rejected the gospel before the rapture could be saved during the tribulation – is one aspect of the series that many dispensationalists find most controversial.[41] A number of on-line discussions, for example, dispute the possibility of a second-chance salvation on the basis of 2 Thessalonians 2:10-11. The idea is certainly controversial.

Second chance theology is, nevertheless, a staple element in the history of the rapture fiction genre, and is presupposed in most of their fictional depictions of the end. *Left Behind* is perhaps

unusual in bringing this matter of controversy into the forefront
of its narrative: 'supposedly lots of preachers believed you couldn't
become a believer after the Rapture. They used that to scare people
into making their decisions in advance.'[42] Now, the novels argue,
the truth is known. There will be a second chance – but only for
a while.

The fear that there is no second chance is a fear that haunts
the characters of the series: 'was there no more mercy, no second chance?'[43] Yet the novels insist that salvation is possible for
those who had already rejected the truth: 'you now have another
chance.'[44] This theology of the second chance challenges the sense
of finality that Christians often attribute to Christ's second coming. But the theology of the second chance is problematic even
within the novel series, because the opportunity of salvation cannot be guaranteed throughout the final seven-year period. During
the tribulation, the opportunity of salvation retreats from individuals even as they become increasingly interested in it. 'If you have
not already rejected him one time too many, you may receive him
now,' one character suggests.[45] But the opportunity of salvation is
decreasing even as the aspiration for salvation grows. The novels
argue that the specific conditions of the tribulation will transform
the relationship between God's sovereignty and human freedom.
Imagine, they suggest, that 'you finally decide it's true and want
to give yourself to Christ, but you had already pushed God past
where he would allow you to come back … the Bible warns about
just that during the end times.'[46]

Effectively, therefore, it is possible that those who desire a
second-chance salvation will find themselves denied it:

"I've been praying that God will save my soul. And when
he does, I will be able to see." Rayford didn't know what
to say. She had said herself it was too late.[47]

"Tell me something then … We don't still have our own
free will?"
    Rayford felt his throat tighten. "Apparently not," he
managed. "I don't quite understand it myself."[48]

Many readers might share Rayford's confusion. At times the series' discussion of the possibility of free will appears baffling. One character worries that 'God may have already hardened your heart so that you could not change your mind if you wanted to';[49] there is no explanation as to how an individual could want something without changing their mind from opposition to it. But the novels insist on this point, even if the language is sometimes obscure: 'That many have already had their hearts hardened by God – a truth that may go against what we once believed about him – is nonetheless clearly the danger of putting off receiving Christ.'[50] That total inability to be saved is finally confirmed when the unbelieving individual submits to the mark of the beast. It is impossible for anyone who takes the mark to later become a believer: 'Scripture was clear that that was a once-and-for-all decision.'[51] Therefore, as far as salvation goes, there is never a better time than the present.

What these quotations attest, therefore, is that the novels have a very peculiar theology of free will. Generally, each individual is left to respond to the offer of salvation at their own discretion. We have already noted that those who are 'dead in trespasses and sins' are somehow enabled to pray the Sinner's Prayer. But as the end times develop, the independence of the human will is overshadowed by a divine curse. The rapidly retreating possibility of salvation is ultimately eclipsed by the new era in human psychology introduced with the mark of the beast. The application of this mark – rather than the second coming of Christ – signals the final division of humanity. The mark of the beast will inaugurate a period of time during which free will is gradually suspended. Believers 'will be *unable* to deny Jesus, *unable* to even choose the mark that would temporarily save our lives'.[52] Unbelievers, those who take the mark, 'will be bound for hell, and even if you want to change your mind, you will not be able to.'[53] Once again, the novels present a curious re-reading of biblical psychology which forgets that the only people who seek after God (Rom. 3:11) are those in whose lives he is already at work.

Rayford knew the prophecy – that people would reject
God enough times that God would harden their hearts
and they wouldn't be able to choose him even if they
wanted to. But knowing it didn't mean Rayford understood it. And it certainly didn't mean he had to like it.
He couldn't make it compute with the God he knew, the
loving and merciful one who seemed to look for ways to
welcome everyone into heaven, not keep them out.[54]

WHERE LEFT BEHIND GOES BADLY WRONG

But these problems pale into insignificance when compared to
the *Left Behind* project's most profound challenge to the biblical
gospel. In *Apocalypse Dawn*, the first instalment of a new series
marketed under the *Left Behind* franchise by the earlier series' publisher, a post-rapture religious revival breaks out among American
troops serving on the Turkish border. One soldier, with pastoral
experience, recovers his sense of vocation and begins to baptise
his colleagues. *Apocalypse Dawn* defines baptism as 'the symbolic
resurrection of a person after accepting the Son of God's most
precious gift', and uses the character of a former Irish Presbyterian
to voice hostility to the practice of infant baptism.[55] Historically,
both those evangelicals adhering to the baptism of believers' children and those who limit baptism to believers only have insisted
that baptism is symbolic either of the salvation the believer already has or of the salvation that the child is promised if they
repent and believe. But, in *Apocalypse Dawn*, this adult baptism
is hardly discussed as being symbolic; instead, it is equated with
actually being 'saved in Christ'.[56] O'Doyle, the Irish Presbyterian
soldier, clearly equates baptism with the experience of salvation,
and, after his baptism, feels 'like I done be reborn', for his baptism
is a process of 'bein' saved in the Lord'.[57] When the soldiers 'decide to get baptized' they 'entrust their souls to God'.[58] *Apocalypse
Dawn* therefore appears to teach a Baptist version of baptismal
regeneration. The novel challenges dispensationalism's normal
assumptions about the validity of the sacraments in the tribulation period, as we will later see, but its serious challenge to the

biblical discussion of salvation surely justifies this chapter's initial citation of Galatians 1. In *Apocalypse Dawn*, the gospel itself is at stake. There could be no clearer signal of the modern evangelical crisis. The project's commitment to historic evangelicalism simply cannot be maintained. Therefore, while the *Left Behind* novels challenge Darby's linking of the rapture to evangelical faith, *Apocalypse Dawn* subverts it altogether. *Apocalypse Dawn* moves far beyond biblical and evangelical truth.

CONCLUSION

Christian writers who have turned to fiction have frequently felt the need to defend their projects from the suspicions of others. John Bunyan began *The Pilgrim's Progress* with a reference to Hosea 12:10: 'I have used Similitudes'. But *Left Behind* has a more problematic fictional method than most. Its sales vastly surpass anything that Christian fiction has ever achieved. It is bringing its distinctive brand of evangelicalism to a wider audience than Christian fiction writers have ever previously addressed, and its authors and publishers are channelling their audience into the four new series that *Left Behind* has spawned. It is right that evangelicals consider the message of the books they entertain.

That kind of consideration shows that the series has a great deal to recommend it. But the *Left Behind* novels, like rapture fictions more generally, emerge from the evangelical subculture to reflect as many of the movement's weaknesses as strengths. The series and its spin-offs demonstrate the significant ways in which theological drift has impacted a once Bible-centred movement. In fact, if these novels are anything to go by, this book's reference to an evangelical 'crisis' might be something of an understatement. With the false hopes of the Sinner's Prayer, the impotence of a not-quite-sufficiently-powerful God, with confusion about the impact and effect of human depravity, and a spin-off novel's suggestion that salvation comes in or through water baptism, it is no wonder that so many evangelical leaders are concerned about the relationship between *Left Behind*, the gospel, and the readers of the sixty million copies the series has sold.

Chapter 5

LEFT BEHIND, THE CHURCH AND THE CHRISTIAN LIFE

"I must clarify that the Scriptures do not refer to us who become believers after the Rapture as Christians. We are referred to as tribulation saints."[1]

PERHAPS THE MOST INTERESTING THING about the quotation with which this chapter begins is that its claim is simply not true. The series repeatedly refers to 'what the Bible calls "tribulation saints"' (note the use of quotation marks), and opts for such alternatives as 'Christ-followers' to avoid applying the term 'Christian' to these post-rapture believers.[2] But surf to any online concordance, search any English Bible translation – even any of the translations quoted in the *Left Behind* series – and you will discover that the expression 'tribulation saints' does not occur anywhere in Scripture. It is used repeatedly in dispensational literature, and is at times almost elevated to biblical status, but there is no suggestion, in the 'precious old King James translation', the translation provided by J. N. Darby, or any Bible translation cited in the series, that those who come to faith during the Antichrist's regime will be known as anything other than Christians.[3] Despite its repeated claims for accuracy, the series gets it wrong.[4]

From one point of view, the question of whether 'tribulation saints' should be called Christians, or should be considered part of the church, might seem extremely trivial. But when millions of readers are delving into the series, and, it seems, being encouraged to uncritically adopt the books as devotional reading, this kind of mistake can wreak disaster.[5] Actually, for reasons we shall see, it matters a great deal whether these post-rapture believers are 'Christians' or members of the church – and all the more so if readers are using these characters to shape the pattern of their lives in the present.

In referring to 'tribulation saints', the *Left Behind* series is following a long tradition in dispensational thought. Classical dispensationalism has always denied that those who are converted after the rapture should be considered as part of the church. This distinction can be traced to the classical dispensational idea that Scripture presents the history and future of not one but two peoples of God, the Christian church and the Jews. Classical dispensationalism insists that there is no overlap between these two groups, and that God's dealings with believing Gentiles in the 'church age' before the rapture should be considered as a 'parenthesis' in his wider plan for the future prosperity of Abraham's physical descendants; as Michael Williams has put it, dispensationalism stands 'in awe of the Jew'.[6] The Gentile church and the ordinances of baptism and the Lord's Supper are only for this age. After the rapture, therefore, with the removal of the Christian church and the end of the parenthesis, the Jewish people would once again be at the centre of divine activity. Those Gentiles who would be converted after the end of the church age would therefore be in a unique situation. These 'tribulation saints' would be neither Jews, nor Christians, nor members of the church.

While the *Left Behind* novels do not share this all-embracing concentration on Jewish themes, they do nevertheless present their believing characters as something other than church-member

Christians. But the novels slip up, and from time to time we see characters describing their fellowship groups in 'church' terms.[7] Rayford, for example, 'just wanted … to be part of this body, this church'.[8] But it is questionable whether the fellowship meetings he refers to are really worthy of the church's name. Without ordinances or any form of church discipline, these meetings exist for fellowship, singing and Bible teaching, and represent a form of discipleship that holds the institutional church in even lower regard than do many expressions of modern evangelicalism. Nevertheless, the novels repeatedly raise the question – 'what is the church?'

Significantly, the fellowship groups described in the series borrow many of their characteristics from the 'cell' structures that have been celebrated in recent church growth literature.[9] As part of their ambition for the total decentralisation of all institutions, the tribulation saints construct 'a vast network of house churches' that they use to frustrate the despotism of the Antichrist's 'Global Community' (the 'GC').[10] Laslos Miklos, facing death by guillotine, encouraged Buck that the cause of Christ could not fail:

> You know our church is made up of many, many small groups that are not so small anymore. When the GC raided the main one, they took my wife and Pastor D and about seventy others, but they missed more than ninety other groups.[11]

The members of these house churches demonstrate astonishing bravery, refusing to disband when history's most evil dictator combines forces with the world's most capable system of enforcement. Undoubtedly they reflect the reality of church life in many lands where Christian worship meetings have been driven underground. But bravery and loyalty do not do away with other central elements of New Testament church life – even when their importance has been dismissed in the modern evangelical crisis.

THE CHURCH AND ITS WORSHIP

One of the most obvious symptoms of the modern evangelical crisis is the collapse of interest in the church. Dispensationalism, by contrast, emerged alongside a rediscovery of the vitality of church life in the communities of early Brethren. Since the early nineteenth century, Brethren writing has been noted for its emphasis on 'church truth'. That emphasis on ecclesiology has disappeared as dispensationalism has been more widely adopted. While parachurch organisations flourish and mega-church growth statistics indicate a seismic change in individual expectations of congregational life, popular evangelicalism often continues to downplay the importance of regulated local fellowship. The novels, emerging from this culture, reflect its ambivalence towards church structures and the privilege of church ordinances. *Left Behind* takes one of the saddest aspects of modern evangelicalism and projects it onto the tribulation period, providing contemporary evangelicals with an image of their own ecclesiastical neglect.

Sadly, many readers of the novels would not realise that its central characters are not, technically, members of the church. Evangelicals have often been notoriously 'low-church', but there does not seem to be a huge distance between the fellowship groups of the tribulation period and many fellowships groups of the present day. The parallel is perhaps most obvious in the series' lack of interest in the church's ordinances. In *Left Behind* and its associated rapture fictions, tribulation saints are represented as meeting together, studying the Bible together, worshipping together, and witnessing together. We have already noted the reasons behind the dispensational teaching that the sacraments are only for the 'church age' – the Lord's Supper, after all, is to be celebrated only 'till he comes' (1 Cor. 11:26). This theological presupposition explains why, with the exception of the new *Apocalypse Dawn* series, rapture fictions do not present the baptism of newly-converted disciples, and explains why the fellowship of believers is not cemented in the sharing of bread and wine. (We have already noted that the baptisms in *Apocalypse Dawn* are exaggerated in their effect, represented as somehow conferring salvation.) *Left Behind* represents believers getting on just fine without observing the ordinances instituted by Jesus Christ.

There are several possible reasons why the novels neglect the ordinances. It is possible that these rapture novels avoid references to the ordinances for reasons of marketing – to prevent being aligned with any particular denomination, an alignment that might serve to limit their wider appeal. In *Apocalypse Dawn*, as we have seen, Mel Odom uses the character of an Irish Presbyterian soldier to mount an attack on the baptism of infants, in a gesture that is unparalleled in the context of the earlier series. But there is also a sense in which this lack of interest in the ordinances is simply a reflection of evangelical church life in the present. Low-church evangelicals have tended to emphasise the practical, and that emphasis has often made them fairly uninterested in the finer details of congregational ordering. Furthermore, their suspicion of the sacramental theology of Roman Catholicism has often encouraged them to embrace an alternative theology that denies any value or faith-based efficacy in the ordinances at all. It is a small step from denying the intrinsic value of the ordinances to ignoring them altogether. But there is even less excuse for this neglect in those rapture novels set before the second coming of Christ. In *Soon*, for example, we see underground fellowships in the 'church age' enjoying worship and Bible study, while avoiding the privileges accorded to the faithful in the proper use of the ordinances. This extremely 'low church' atmosphere allows the narrative to continue its fast pace without pausing to explain or choose between the theologies of infant or adult baptism, for example – and therefore allows the narrative to carry the sympathies of a wide range of Christian readers.

But there is grave danger in this neglect. The ordinances were not given to the church because they are of no value. There is great merit in considering them as means of grace, channels through which God communicates grace to his people when they share in the ordinances with faith in Jesus Christ. The sacraments are the marks of covenant membership: baptism, with its once-for-all marking of inclusion in the church, and the Lord's Supper, as a regular rite of remembrance. Dispensationalists would be uncomfortable with the idea of their being 'in covenant', as a great deal of their literature describes the New Covenant as something uniquely for millennial Israel. Neither would they argue that the ordinances can be means of fellowship with Christ when the tribulation saints are neither Christians nor a part of his Body. The question of whether the novels' central characters are in fact in union with Christ is never fully addressed – yet its implications are enormous. It is strange that the series' characters can sing 'Amazing Grace' at the same time as they neglect a means by which that grace is communicated.[12]

THE CHURCH AND THE WORLD

Rapture fictions, therefore, underplay the significance of the church, its continuing status as the Body of Christ, and the importance of its means of grace, both in the 'church age' and in the tribulation. At the same time, however, rapture fictions also reconfigure the church's relationship with the world.

Christians, as the motto goes, are to be in the world without being of it. The statement is often erroneously attributed to Jesus Christ, but is an accurate summary of his teaching in passages like John 17. The tension between being in the world yet not of the world is a tension that drives Christian discipleship. The tension forces Christians to weigh up their often competing responsibilities as family members, church members, employees and citizens. It's no surprise that believers often get it wrong. Sometimes believers have tried to be in the world and of the world; that is evidence of spiritual decay. At other times believers have tried to be of the world, yet not in the world; that has been evidence of hypocritical separatism. It is easier to retreat from the world, or to abandon oneself to it entirely. But Christians are to embrace the tension. Being in the world allows Christians to love their neighbours as themselves. Being in the world without being of the world allows Christians to love God while loving their neighbours as themselves.

The characters in *Left Behind*, like many Christians in the real world, struggle to maintain both sides of that balance. In part, the struggle is generated by the narrative situation of the novels. By focusing on the final period of tribulation, and by drawing their characters from a group of tribulation saints that dispensational theology insists are not part of the church, these rapture fictions depict believers in opposition to and in retreat from a world of overwhelming and irredeemable evil. Occasionally it is possible to see individuals snatched as 'brands from the burning', but the overall message of rapture fictions is that it is impossible to bring reformation to the world, and any attempt to do so is futile.

There is therefore little room in the novels for social concern. With the world in disarray, a concern for individual survival overcomes a ministry to the needy modelled on the incarnation of Jesus Christ. The tribulation saints face the full blast of persecution:

> Any cult, sect, religion, or individual who professes a single avenue to God or heaven or bliss in the afterlife is the greatest danger to the global community. Such a view engenders divisiveness, hatred, bigotry, condescension, and pride.[13]

Instead of challenging their enemies' preconceptions, however, the tribulation saints respond to these fears by arming themselves and retreating from the hostile world. They choose to love God instead of loving their neighbour. But believers in every age are required to do both, for they have a duty to the world just as they have a duty to their God, a duty that involves service alongside witness. It is almost irrelevant whether that service incurs a painful cost. The life of the believer continues under the cross.

By using the 'tribulation saints' as a model for contemporary church life, therefore, the *Left Behind* series, like rapture fiction more generally, underplays the significance of ecclesiology, worship, and other aspects of the Christian life. Whatever the consensus of the rapture fictions, tribulation saints are not a category of believers identified in the Bible as distinct from the church. Believers, in every age, are part of the church and are commanded to make regular use of whatever ordinances God has provided for their age. It is impossible to find biblical support for the notion that believers can grow in grace while ignoring the means of grace that God has provided. In the New Testament age, Christians are the Body of Christ, in union with Christ, and enjoy the benefits of that union through the means of grace that the Head of the Body has appointed. Never, at any time, can believers begin to suspect they can progress without the ordinances their Saviour instituted.

That's why rapture fictions do not present a healthy model for church life – even for church life in the last days. To the end of the age, the relationship between Jesus Christ and his people cannot change – they will still be in union with him, and will still enjoy the benefits of that union by the means of grace he has appointed. And the believer's relationship to the world will not change, even in the conditions of incomparable persecution that Scripture certainly predicts and the church increasingly experiences. Christians are not to be of the world, for they are to love God with all their heart, soul, body and mind. But Christians are to be in the world, for there is never any alternative to humble, loving service – even suffering service under the cross.

Left Behind and the Christian life

It is possible that another explanation of the novels' neglect of the church is to be found in their celebration of the individual. Like so much of modern evangelicalism, the novels elevate the individual above the collective life of the church, and, at times, invest (and so defend) that individualism with an almost mystical spirituality.

In a sense, this unusual mysticism is related to one of the novels' least satisfactory fictional elements. Throughout the series, 'God seems to be working in much more direct and dramatic ways all the time.'[14] The increasing possibility of the unusual actually works to the detriment of the novels' fictional technique. There is little call for inventive plotting when the authors can simply invoke the impossible on the basis that miracles will increase as the end of the age draws near. In *Desecration* (2001), for example, the Jewish remnant waiting at Petra is protected from an assaulting army. As the tanks bear down upon them, Rayford imagines that the remnant's escape will be made possible by a miracle: 'This flood from the serpent's mouth was going to hit an invisible wall or be swept away by some wall of water from nowhere, or the Israelis and their helpers would prove so ethereal that the weapons of destruction would pass harmlessly through them.' Instead, 'the earth split and ripped open for a mile in every direction', and the army fell into a 'colossal gorge that appeared to reach the bowels of hell'.[15] Later, in the same book, the Jewish remnant at Petra is fed with manna and quail, and drink 'fresh, cool water' that springs miraculously from the rocks, like their Old Testament counterparts in the days of Moses.[16]

The plausibility of the impossible – even the expectation of the impossible – is developed in the novels' presentation of the Christian life. The novels promote a mystical individualism which bears little resemblance to the normal experiences of New Testament believers. Without explaining their novelty, the novels insist that elements of this mystical experience are available to believers in every age, and will grow increasingly common as the end approaches. Tsion Ben-Judah, a former Rabbi and Israeli statesman, makes rapid progress in mastering the techniques of late-twentieth-century American evangelicalism after his conversion to evangelical faith:

> Tsion had studied the discipline of intercession, largely a Protestant tradition from the fundamentalist and Pentecostal cultures. Those steeped in it went beyond mere praying for someone as an act of interceding for them; they believed true intercession involved deep empathy and that a person thus praying must not enter into the practice unless willing to literally trade places with the needy person.[17]

There is little need to comment on the idea of 'tradition' in 'fundamentalist and Pentecostal cultures' – Pentecostal and fundamentalist readers might be astonished and appalled to discover they were guilty of having any tradition at all! Nevertheless, there is something going on here that is too close to the 'psychobabble' the novels elsewhere appropriately condemn.[18] Tsion is faithful in evaluating his spiritual experiences by Scripture, but his ministry of intercession generates several 'out-of-body experiences' that he struggles to understand.[19]

However we assess these experiences, the novels are making a serious point about the nature of evangelical spirituality. But while Tsion's experiences may reflect trends common in certain Pentecostal or fundamentalist cultures, there is little attempt to root these experiences in Scripture. Of course, it is true that biblical praying could involve these kinds of experiences. Paul, caught up to the third heaven, heard things that he could not express (2 Cor. 12:4). But his account of the experience also emphasised that it was an incredibly unusual event, and he didn't confirm or deny that it took place outside the body (v. 2). He certainly did not suggest that this was a normal part of New Testament spirituality. Here again, the novels' narrative form may be working against the careful and balanced articulation of biblical truth. By this stage in the series, readers have been regularly primed to anticipate the unusual, and the unusual must be continually provided for readers to keep turning the page. If that is the case, it might be that the demands of the genre have outweighed the demands of truth. The novels' spirituality might then owe more to the entertaining and experience-orientated spirit of the age than to the sanctifying and empowering Spirit of God.

Even when the novels do concentrate on authentic spirituality, the benefits of collective worship are overwhelmed by this deference to individual experience. Tsion felt a 'tingle' that preceded his out-of-body experience.[20] While the Bible contains nothing that would suggest such 'tingling' was normal, the novels' presentation of evangelical spirituality repeatedly emphasises the importance of physical senses and emotions. After a series of trials, for example, Rayford 'believed he had made intimate contact with God ..., had communicated more directly, and felt more personally connected to heaven than he had in ages'.[21] Notice the language: 'intimate contact', 'communicated more directly', 'felt more personally connected'. This is the language of romance, never unusual in mystical literature, but highly unusual in New Testament spirituality. The tribulation saints are absolutely in touch with their emotions. Buck, who 'had already fallen in love with God,' noticed lots of hugging on his first visit to the fellowship – 'especially among the men'.[22] Rayford's language of 'intimate contact' is an attempt to get God to join in.

Left Behind and guidance

This movement away from strict biblicism finds its counterpart in the characters' search for spiritual guidance. Here again, the novels show some flexibility in negotiating with the culture from which they have emerged. Dispensationalism insists that believers before and after the rapture will follow fundamentally different patterns for holy behaviour. Before the rapture, Christians, existing in the 'parenthesis' of the 'church age', are not under any element of Old Testament law, or even responsible to obey the moral teachings of Jesus Christ; instead, they are to find their moral compass in the epistles of Paul. After the rapture, with the end of the 'church parenthesis' and with the rekindling of God's interest in the Jews, believers will again be under law, finding direction both in the commandments of the Old Testament and in the Sermon on the Mount. (Some more marginal dispensationalists go further, we have noticed, even claiming that law-keeping will be part of the way of salvation during the tribulation period.) But these expectations, long defended by classical dispensationalists, are frustrated in *Left Behind*.

In fact, the *Left Behind* novels move quite some distance from the mainstream, classical dispensational tradition when they present their characters as not being under any law at all. Rayford, for example, considers whether his killing of Carpathia should actually be considered murder. Biblically, there is little doubt that it could be anything else. The Ten Commandments, as well as the Sermon on the Mount, make clear that anything from unjustified anger to physical assault should be considered a violation of this prohibition, and nothing in Scripture suggests that the prohibition will be relaxed as the end of the age approaches. But Rayford doesn't consider this, and his lack of attention to Scriptural guidance confirms the series' wider displacement of biblical norms. When Buck and Chloe fall in love, similarly, they wonder about the propriety of marriage and family life in the world's last and most terrible years. Bruce Barnes, the earliest pastor of the Tribulation Force, researches the topics of courtship and marriage in the tribulation period, but dies before he gets to present his conclusions. Buck and Chloe discuss the situation and search for guidance without any extended reference to God's Word. It is as if passages like 1 Corinthians 7 had lost their moral authority during the tribulation period. A character in *Apocalypse Dawn* sums up this new approach: 'the best way to know what God wanted in a person's life was by paying attention to the small niggling doubts that often turned into guilt if left unchecked.'[23] Throughout the

Left Behind project, subjectivity and intuition are elevated over objectivity and the written word. Characters do what they 'feel' is God's will, not only what they find as guidance in the Bible.

There is a sense in which the series is compelled to mount these challenges on classical dispensational belief. From a dispensational point of view, tribulation-saint characters who find guidance in the Ten Commandments or the Sermon on the Mount would be unacceptable as models of Christian behaviour for believers in the present. But by imagining such tribulation saints as paying no heed to the law, the series dismisses the value of the law, in its entirety, for either of dispensationalism's two peoples of God.

Perhaps it is this neglect of the law that most clearly demonstrates the series' distance from both classical dispensationalism and the historic evangelical faith. Dispensationalism insists that tribulation saints are under the moral law, while believers in the current age are not. Historic evangelical theology insists that all believers in every age are under the moral law: Christ redeems us from the curse of the law in our salvation, and sends us back to the law to see our pattern for holy behaviour.[24] But the novels go far beyond what critics of dispensationalism have often opposed to suggest that guidance is subjective and intuitive as often as it is biblical. This living by intuition is hardly living by faith. A theology of Christian living that is not governed by the moral law of God is a frightening possibility. On what basis, other than the Bible, can we properly know God's will?

LEFT BEHIND AND THE AUTHORITY OF TRUTH

It is ironic that this denial of the value of the law of God is paralleled by an exaggeration of the value of individual opinion – but if it is ironic, it is hardly surprising. The Christian life needs an authoritative foundation, and if it does not find it in Scripture it will find it somewhere else. Not many believers are satisfied with a theology that is more clearly rooted in the individual's imagination that in some external source. The same is true of the characters in *Left Behind*, and the series goes on to suggest what form that external source might take. In *Left Behind*, as in many evangelical cultures, the liberty that is found in the law of God is replaced by the authoritative statements of a leader who insists that his word is unchanging truth.

Perhaps the most serious of all the series' claims is its insistence on the absolute certainty of the prophetic perspective it endorses. Characters are certainly right when they insist on the importance and applicability of prophecy:

> nearly 30 per cent of the Bible (Old and New Testaments together) consisted of prophetic passages. I could not understand why God would include these if he intended them to be other than understandable to his children.[25]

The novels voice justified frustration at the number of evangelicals who fail to consider the import of Bible prophecy. But the series swings too far to the opposite extreme. Instead of ignoring prophecy, it identifies its own prophetic perspective as eternally unchanging truth, and claims that its version of dispensationalism is the only accurate understanding of the end.

That certainty begins to overstate itself when characters parallel the details of their convictions with the reliability of Scripture itself. Tsion, for example, goes too far when he concludes a prophetic sermon with an astonishing claim for his own infallibility: 'If this does not happen, label me a heretic or mad and look elsewhere than the Holy Scriptures for hope.'[26]

It is this insistent certainty that makes *Left Behind* – like so many other rapture fictions – such a menace to the Christian church. Admitting no possibility of error, the novels' characters identify their own words with the infallibility that belongs only to the Word of God. This is overweening pride, and the history of the church is littered with prophetic 'experts' who similarly staked their reputations on the unfounded conclusions of prophetic study. But the novels go beyond that, and stake the reputation and credibility of Scripture itself on the accuracy of their predictions. This is a gross manipulation of truth.

Whatever some may claim for the literal fulfilment of prophecy, it is clear that many of the prophecies of the first coming of Christ were not understood until after the event. That being the case, it is difficult to imagine what could make anyone believe that detailed prophecies of his second coming would be any easier to understand. What could make anyone so self-confident of their interpretation of the most difficult passages in Scripture that they would be prepared to abandon Scripture if their interpretations were disproved?

Prophecy, someone has suggested, either finds a man mad or leaves him so. Tsion, it appears, has committed the ultimate folly, so closely identifying his own conclusions with Scripture that the authority of the latter is lost when the conclusions of the former are undermined. 'Let him that thinketh he standeth take heed lest he fall' (1 Cor. 10:12), for we know nothing yet as we ought to know (1 Cor. 8:2). When readers begin to reject the authority of Scripture because Tsion's expectations are not confirmed, the recklessness of his statement will become clear. Far from defending the authority of Scripture, he has grounded its credibility on the unstable foundation of his own intellectual prowess. If he falls into error, he has ensured that God's reputation will fall with him.

Of course, the novels are full of congratulations for those wise enough to have been dispensationalists in advance. The novels imagine that the rapture would confirm the error of those who adopted alternative explanations of the end, and send them running for the truth:

> Many were confused before the rapture of the church and believed that the apostle Paul's second letter to the Thessalonians referred to that event when he spoke of "the coming of our Lord Jesus Christ and our gathering together to him." … it is now clear that Paul was speaking of the Glorious Appearing.[27]

Cannot the same change of opinion be expected if the rapture does not occur before the tribulation? And, if believers have been taught that the pre-tribulation rapture is absolutely the teaching of Scripture, will they not abandon the Bible along with their dispensationalism, and, as Tsion argued, 'look elsewhere for hope'? Our prophetic conclusions are never infallible until they have been confirmed. Far from upholding the authority of Scripture, and the humility of interpretation, the novels have provided an opportunity for the future ridicule that could yet drive many from the faith.

CONCLUSION

This chapter has presented a serious claim – that the *Left Behind* novels are seriously deficient in their views of the church and the Christian life, and that they exemplify the common evangelical failing of substituting an alternative human authority for the authority of God's law. Their account of the displacement of Scripture, and its replacement by 'traditions' and teachers who cannot distinguish between the authority of their own conclusions and the authority of God, is another symptom of the crisis that challenges the future of the evangelical church. It cannot be disputed that the series represents an evangelical phenomenon. But it must be feared that the series represents a substantial break with historic evangelical beliefs. There are serious issues with *Left Behind* and its theology of the church and the Christian life.

Chapter 6

THE BIBLE AND THE FUTURE OF HUMANITY

'This script has already been written. I have read it. You lose.'[1]

WHATEVER THE PROBLEMS WE MIGHT SEE in *Left Behind*, or in rapture fiction more generally, the novels are right about this – Jesus Christ is coming back.

In its best days, the church has never doubted this. Throughout the New Testament, and in the days of the apostolic fathers, Christian writers insisted that, at the end of history, Jesus Christ would return to earth to resurrect the dead, judge the world, and establish a kingdom for his people. As the church grew in power and prestige, however, the hope of the imminence of Christ's return began to fade. Expectations of earthly glory and political power obscured the brightness of the 'blessed hope' (Titus 2:13). But, even in those dark days, the thought of the return of Christ was always a part of Christian orthodoxy. Today, across the world, while the church is torn apart by schism and confusion, millions of people continue to recite the words of the Apostles' Creed, restating their belief that the risen Jesus Christ, who has ascended into heaven, 'will come to judge the quick and the dead'.

It is that sense of finality, of an ultimate reckoning, that seems to offend so many of those who have written about the *Left Behind* phenomenon. A great deal of the thinking of our modern world is rooted in a pluralism that accepts almost anything so long as it does not harm or offend anyone else. The thought that every individual's life will be punished or rewarded according to eternally unchanging standards is, to many cheerful modern pluralists, extremely offensive. Nevertheless, when secular critics ridicule the writers of rapture fiction for their belief that Jesus' return will have immense implications for the whole of humanity, their ridicule is directed at all orthodox Christians, not just the purveyors of a curious and theologically short-sighted American fictional series.

THE CHURCH AND THE END OF THE WORLD

No one who takes Scripture seriously can doubt its emphasis on the second coming of Jesus Christ. James Montgomery Boice, the esteemed American Presbyterian minister, calculated that one verse in every twenty-five in the New Testament referred to Jesus Christ's return, with 318 mentions in its 260 chapters.[2] But, as anyone knows who has spent any time reflecting on the biblical teaching, there are many quite different ways of understanding what this emphasis actually means.

This variety of explanation suggests one reason why so many evangelicals do not live in the expectation of Christ's second coming. Tragically, many of them have been told they do not have to. Many of those who have been educated in environments influenced by post-millennialism have been instructed that Christ's coming cannot occur within their lifetimes, for the thousand-year period that precedes Christ's second coming (which they find in Revelation 20) may not yet have properly begun. Others who have been educated in environments influenced by the recently-revived preterism (a system of interpretation that finds the fulfilment of a great deal of Bible prophecy in the fall of Jerusalem in

A.D. 70) have been told not to look for Christ's coming, for, in some senses, it has already happened.[3] Other evangelical environments are more noted for their disdain for dispensationalism or pre-millennialism than for their own bright advent hope. Despite its repeated affirmations of faith, therefore, the evangelical church has not always lived with the expectation of Jesus' coming. Those believers who criticise *Left Behind* should ensure that they are as enthusiastic as the novels about promoting a vision of Christian living grounded in the expectation of the Lord's return.

The last thing this book should do is discourage anyone from being serious about the expectation of the 'blessed hope'. There are aspects of rapture fiction that should cause evangelicals serious concern, and it is right that fellow evangelicals should look at the series, testing all things and holding on to what is good (1 Thess. 5:21). The same scrutiny should be extended to this book, and all the others that challenge the *Left Behind* worldview. No Christian is exempt, and no Christian should expect to be exempt, from brotherly criticism and challenge. Nothing that this book argues, therefore, should be understood as playing down the unparalleled significance of the fact that Jesus Christ will soon return to the earth. But this book does argue that evangelicals influenced by popular rapture fictions should re-think what his coming will involve in the future and what it requires in the present.

THE WORLD, THE CHURCH, AND THE END

Todd Strandberg is one of the world's most unusual men. By day, he fixes planes on an air base in Nebraska. By night, he is the webmaster of the Rapture Index, which he describes as a 'Dow Jones average of end-times activity', a 'prophetic speedometer'.[4] Instead of stocks and shares, the Rapture Index tracks Strandberg's understanding of the fulfilment of prophecies – earthquakes, plagues, floods, crime, false prophets and economic unrest – anything that might be seen to pave the way for the Antichrist. The Rapture Index always points to one question – just how close are we to the end of the age?

For many years the prophetic concern promoted by Strandberg would have been dismissed by the wider world as utter lunacy. But the 9-11 attack on the World Trade Centre raised the profile of his website so much that by 24 September 2001 the Rapture Index had attracted a staggering eight million visitors. The events of September 2001 triggered a 'rapture ready' reading that was not even equalled by the devastation caused by the Asian tsunami of December 2004.[5] That astonishing response was part of a much wider cultural movement which suggests that the world – or, at least, the American world – has suddenly re-discovered its sense of apocalypse. At the beginning of the twentieth century, the poet T. S. Eliot wrote that the world would end 'not with a bang but a whimper'.[6] No-one believes that anymore.

But there are many within the church that would prefer it to be true. Within evangelicalism there are many who would rather oppose the apocalyptic visions of *Left Behind* than develop their own bright advent hope. Ironically, in its new fascination with the end, the world has turned to what many parts of the church appear to have forgotten.

The New Testament writers anticipated this trend. 2 Peter warns its readers that the church's neglect of biblical prophecy will itself be a 'sign of the times'. In his first letter, Peter had warned the young churches of pressures from outside their fellowship. In his second letter, his attention turned to dangers that would emerge from inside their memberships. The letter warns of false teachers who would come to trouble the church with their mocking denial that Jesus Christ would come again: 'where is the promise of his coming?' (2 Peter 3:4).

There are many reasons for neglecting biblical prophecy. Perhaps the most basic is fear: it is a profoundly frightening thing to consider the heavens being dissolved, being on fire, and the elements melting with fervent heat (2 Peter 3:12). You can see that kind of cosmic violence illustrated in one of the most powerful images of eschatological disaster, *The opening of the sixth seal* (1824), by the Irish painter Francis Danby. Not long after it was finished, Danby hung the painting in an exhibition in London. One night, a vandal crept in and slashed out the picture's central image – a freed slave, standing with his arms uplifted and chains dangling from his wrists, with a king fallen before him, his crown knocked from his head. The political implications of the end of the age were just too much for this socially-conservative vandal, who must have been profoundly frightened by the insignificance of wealth, power and social hierarchy on the day when the 'kings of the earth, and the great men, and the rich men, and the chief captains, and the mighty men, and every bondman, and every free man' will beg the mountains to hide them from the 'wrath of the Lamb' (Rev. 6:15-16). But the same trend is present in certain evangelical circles. Fear of the awesome and devastating implications of the apocalypse keep many from a study of its description in Scripture.

It is also possible that many Christians avoid the subject of Bible prophecy because they have seen the terrible divisions that an enthusiasm for prophetic study can bring. Far from promoting godly living, those who have grown most interested in biblical prophecy have sometimes also been the least enthusiastic to promote the unity of God's people, fostering divisions over apparently obscure details of apocalyptic interpretation. Other Christians may avoid prophetic study because of its potential for distraction: the sad spectacle of the prophetic 'expert' who contributed nothing to the life of his church was once too common a stereotype. Thankfully there may now be fewer of those who are 'too heavenly minded to be of any earthly use', as the cliché once inaccurately put it. But many others avoid prophetic study simply because it all seems too confusing. They listen to one sermon, and feel persuaded by its contents; then listen to another, which they find equally persuasive, and are astonished to discover that the two contradict.

Armed with these excuses for ignorance, too few modern Christians would be concerned if the preaching to which they were listening never referred to the second coming of Jesus Christ. In some circles within evangelicalism that omission is seen as a mark of theological – even 'Reformed' – respectability. Tragically, evangelicals too often distance themselves from an absorbing interest in the Second Coming when they want to distance themselves from the most obvious of fundamentalism's extremes.

But Peter warns that this denial of the importance of Christ's second coming is the thin end of a dangerous wedge. With the relegation of prophecy comes a new approach to ethics: the false teachers he anticipated will walk according to their own lusts (2 Peter 3:3), denying the reality of any ultimate reckoning. Their relegation of prophecy will promote an equally dangerous approach to the understanding of history. The false teachers will advocate a closed universe, a universe in which everything is understandable on the basis of naturalistic cause and effect, a universe in which God does not intervene: 'since the fathers fell asleep, all things continue as they were from the beginning of the creation' (3:4).

That sentiment may sound familiar – it is the very foundation of the mainstream secular, scientific worldview. But Peter does not commend these false teachers for their intellectual prowess. Instead, he argues, their arguments illustrate wilful ignorance (3:5), a deliberate forgetting that God created the world by his Word and water (3:5), that God judged the world by his Word and water (3:6), and that God will yet destroy the world by his Word and fire (3:7). 'Reserved for fire' might be the motto written above the greatest achievements of the human race (3:7).

Confronted with the shocking fact that 'all these things shall be dissolved' (3:11), evangelicals have no acceptable excuse for prophetic apathy. The difficulty of the material is no excuse for ignorance, for biblical prophecy was even more difficult to understand in the first century than it is now. The first believers found themselves living at the apex of the Old Testament promises. Many of the events that the Hebrew Scriptures appeared to date to the end of the age had been fulfilled in their very recent past. In many ways it seemed that the new world had already begun. The resurrection of the dead had already happened, Christ being the first-fruits of those that sleep (1 Cor. 15:20). Similarly, the last-days outpouring of the Holy Spirit, predicted by Joel, had been witnessed by believing Jews from many lands on the day of Pentecost (Acts 2:1-39). Perhaps a famous statement of Jesus Christ would have been the most confusing of all – what did he mean when he insisted that 'this generation shall not pass [away], till all these things be fulfilled' (Matt. 24:34)? The apostolic generation was passing away – Peter, after all, was writing to them about his death (2 Peter 1:14-15) – but still the Lord had not returned. What could be the explanation for his delay? In the midst of their confusion, Peter wrote to remind them, on the basis of God's promise, to look for new heavens and a new earth, in which righteousness dwells (2 Peter 3:13).

A FUTURE OF HOPE

This hope for a new earth, a righteous earth, is not something that is unique to evangelical Christians. Marxists, trusting in the inexorable laws of history, expect to witness the rise of the international proletariat and an end to economic exploitation. Islamic revolutionaries, trusting in their duty of *jihad*, work for a world under the control of Islamic law. Christians also hope for a new earth, but on quite a different basis. Its coming is certain – not because of the inexorable laws of history, nor the duty of violent conquest, but because of the unshakable promises of God.

This hope for the future is rooted in the writings of the past. Peter referred his readers to prophecies recorded in the Old Testament, the 'words ... spoken before by the holy prophets' (2 Peter 3:2). These would be words like those in Isaiah 65:17-19:

> For, behold, I create new heavens and a new earth: and the former shall not be remembered, nor come into mind. But be ye glad and rejoice for ever in that which I create: for, behold, I create Jerusalem a rejoicing, and her people a joy. And I will rejoice in Jerusalem, and joy in my people: and the voice of weeping shall be no more heard in her, nor the voice of crying.

They might also be words like these, in Isaiah 66:22-24:

> For as the new heavens and the new earth, which I will make, shall remain before me, saith the LORD, so shall your seed and your name remain. And it shall come to pass, that from one new moon to another, and from one sabbath to another, shall all flesh come to worship before me, saith the LORD. And they shall go forth, and look upon the carcases of the men that have transgressed against me: for their worm shall not die, neither shall their fire be quenched; and they shall be an abhorring unto all flesh.

Peter was also able to refer his readers to writings that would be included in the New Testament, 'the commandment of us, the apostles of the Lord and Saviour' (2 Peter 3:2). John wrote these words in Revelation 21:1-5:

> And I saw a new heaven and a new earth: for the first heaven and the first earth were passed away; and there was no more sea. And I John saw the holy city, new Jerusalem, coming down from God out of heaven, prepared as a bride adorned for her husband. And I heard a great voice out of heaven saying, Behold, the tabernacle of God is with men, and he will dwell with them, and they shall be his people, and God himself shall be with them, and be their God. And God shall wipe away all tears from their eyes; and there shall be no more death, neither sorrow, nor crying, neither shall there be any more pain: for the former things are passed away. And he that sat upon the throne said, Behold, I make all things new.

Remarkably, it might seem, in a context of apostasy, when the future of Christian witness in Asia Minor seemed profoundly uncertain, Peter encouraged the believers to take an interest in prophecy. The duty of Christians in the midst of a threatening world was to remember the glory of the future – their future.

Nevertheless, the existence of apostasy demonstrated that the new world had not yet arrived. Two worlds appeared to co-exist – the Christian's tensions between flesh and spirit found their cosmic counterpart in the struggle between the kingdoms of darkness and light. Nevertheless, the final victory of the righteous was sure. Peter wrote of a full-scale cosmological revolution, in which the maturing life of the new world required the final destruction of the old. It would involve the transformation of the heavens and earth (2 Peter 3:7), with a 'great noise' and 'fervent heat' (3:10); the judgement of the spiritual world (the 'elements' in 3:10 are not earth, wind, fire and water, but the spiritual forces struggling for the control of the created order); the judgement of individuals, and the final 'perdition of ungodly men' (3:7). But Peter also suggests what will happen when that judgement is complete. As a character in *Desecration* puts it, 'This script has already been written. I have read it. You lose.'[7]

THAT FUTURE COULD INCLUDE YOU

It is no light thing to lose the glory of the future world. But entry into the new heaven and earth is not without its demands. The new heavens and new earth will be the home of righteousness, Peter insists (3:13), and that righteousness is made known to individuals in the present. While many people will doubtless wake up in the next world astonished to discover themselves in hell, the Bible gives no indication that anyone will be surprised to find themselves in the world that Peter describes. The reason for this is that those people who are heading for glory in the future are being made ready for that glory in the present.

We do not know when Jesus Christ will return, except that for the unprepared his return will be as sudden and unexpected as a 'thief in the night' (3:10). He himself refers to the idea of suddenness three times: once, in Luke 12:39-40, in the parable of the unfaithful steward, and twice in Revelation (3:3; 16:15). It will be a day of awesome horror: the pain and shock reflected in Danby's vandalised painting gives only a hint of what is ultimately an utterly unimaginable event.

But believers will be ready, so that the Day will not overtake them like a thief (1 Thess. 5:4). These will be those who are being made ready for the new world in the present. But they are not building bunkers, or collecting gold – the survival strategies that many defended as they waited for the devastation of Y2K have no counterpart as we wait for God's final confrontation with sin. Preparation for that day is spiritual and moral – not physical or material. The people who are being made ready for this new world are being made holy (3:11), and they are being made expectant, 'looking for and hastening unto the coming of the day of God' (3:12). But the people of the new world are not yet perfect, either morally or numerically. God is delaying that final day, for he is patient for repentance. He waits for the repentance of believers (3:9), and he waits for the repentance of those of his elect who are not yet believers (3:15; 2 Tim. 2:10).

There is, therefore, an answer to the question of why history continues. Throughout the passage, Peter is explaining the meaning of history. His critics said that God was negligent, or careless, 'slack concerning his promise' (3:9). But Peter said that God's purposes stood, and that the continuation of history proved that God was patient, longing for repentance (3:15). These two attitudes to meaning in history find their parallel in the chapter's two contrasting attitudes to the second coming of Jesus Christ: we can reject it, like the false teachers and all those since who have downplayed its significance (3:4); or we can 'look for' it, like all those whom God is fashioning for the last and future world (3:12). Do you 'look for' it?

This kind of individual action is absolutely necessary, for one of the most significant themes in 2 Peter 3 is reflected in something that it does not say. The message of this letter – like the rest of Scripture – is not that the world can escape destruction if it repents. Instead, the message of Scripture is that the world is doomed, but that individuals can escape its destruction if they put their trust in Jesus Christ. Every reader of 2 Peter 3 is left to choose between two worlds and two destinies, summed up in two competing attitudes to the second coming of Jesus Christ. There is a choice to be made. Choose wisely, so that you, according to his promise, can look for a new heavens and new earth, in which righteousness dwells forever.

THE GOSPEL AND THE END OF THE WORLD

Inevitably, therefore, the thought of the second coming returns us to the Christian gospel – and that is always how it should be. 'The testimony of Jesus is the spirit of prophecy' (Rev. 19:10), and prophetic study must always return to the cross.

It is little wonder that the greatest of England's Victorian preachers, C. H. Spurgeon, grew impatient at the antics of those of his contemporaries whose fascination with prophecy led them away from the gospel:

> Your guess at the number of the beast, your Napoleonic speculations, your conjectures concerning a personal Antichrist – forgive me, I count them but mere bones for

dogs; while men are dying, and hell is filling, it seems to me the veriest drivel to be muttering about an Armageddon at Sebastopol or Sadowa or Sedan, and peeping between the folded leaves of destiny to discover the fate of Germany.[8]

While souls are dying, the gospel is paramount, and systems of prophecy are accurate and useful insofar as they support and elevate the gospel's claims. It is salutary to remember that a person can be right in their understanding of every prophetic detail and still end up in hell.

That is why it is much too simple to argue that the greatest danger of the rapture novels is the distraction of a misleading eschatology. That has always been a convenient argument for those who want to illustrate the follies of dispensationalism. And that certainly seems to be one purpose of the recent publication of an alternative rapture novel – the first of a projected series of four – designed to advance a more traditionally 'Reformed' prophetic perspective. Ironically, and controversially, these novels are published by Tyndale House, the same publisher that produced the original *Left Behind* series. Media reports have spoken of LaHaye's feeling of 'betrayal' at the news: 'They are going to take the money we made for them and promote this nonsense', *Christian Retailing* reported him as stating. He might have good reason for concern: while *Left Behind* sold 85,000 copies in its first year of publication, Tyndale House noted that the first instalment of *The Last Disciple*, by Hank Hanegraaff and Sigmund Brouwer, sold 50,000 copies in its first six weeks.[9]

But the successful marketing of an alternative eschatology will not address the most serious problems the earlier rapture fictions raise. What evangelicals need above everything else is a reconsideration of the gospel, a reconsideration that takes us away from the accretions of the venerable traditions of old-time, fundamental religion, a revolution that takes us back to the great reformation banner of 'Scripture alone'.

What the rapture fictions demonstrate, therefore, is that evangelicalism has comprehensively failed. In a sense, these rapture fictions are only too 'evangelical' – they reflect too closely the problems and tensions in the modern, Western evangelical church. But simultaneously, they are not nearly 'evangelical' enough – as their statements on the gospel, the church and the Christian life suggest, the novels have lost sight of what it was that drove the reformation, of the doctrine that has ballasted God's people throughout the history of the church. Above all else, rapture fictions demonstrate that evangelicalism has entered serious crisis, that it has lost sight of the gospel which once gave the evangelical movement its name. And that needn't be the case. J. N. Darby is just one of a number of dispensational leaders who could show the rapture novelists a way to combine their particular eschatology with a vibrant and steadfast evangelical hope – while there is still an opportunity for change.

CONCLUSION

By now, the main themes of this book should be clear. *Left Behind*, despite its remarkable success, is a symptom of an unhealthy evangelicalism. The earlier series and its more recent spin-offs outline an inadequate account of the gospel, presenting as the content of saving faith something quite different from the message preached by the apostles. The novels are uncertain about the purpose of the church, the importance of the sacraments, and the life of the Christian under the law and under the cross. *Left Behind* – like much of the evangelicalism that celebrates its success – is the product of a shrinking theology.

If this conclusion is accurate, it makes possible what may be an astonishing claim – that what is now known as 'evangelicalism' is something qualitatively different from that which the term once described. This conclusion suggests that evangelicalism itself now requires reformation, a reformation that will take it back to Scripture, away from the accretions of tradition that have been institutionalised over centuries. This conclusion suggests that a great deal of modern evangelicalism is now no more governed by Scripture than was much of the thinking of the medieval church it once rejected.

If this modern evangelicalism has lost sight of the contents of the gospel, is unsure about the purpose of the church, has no appreciation of the significance of the sacraments, can imagine a life of faith without God's law or suffering under Christ's cross, it is an evangelicalism unworthy of the name. More seriously, it is an evangelicalism unworthy of the Saviour. That is the tragedy of *Left Behind* – and the devastating consequence of the wider evangelical crisis.

Chapter 7

ESCHATOLOGY AND EVANGELICAL RENEWAL

'How far would God let this go before sending the conquering King?'[1]

THERE IS SOMETHING STRANGELY NOSTALGIC about the futuristic genre of rapture fiction. As much as the novels are about the opportunities of the future, or the problems of the present, they are about the eclipse of the values of the past. The past, in the novels, is a better world, one far removed from the declension of the present:

> "I mean, this is still America, isn't it?"
> "Not the one I remember."[2]

This sense of regret, of longing for a lost world, drives the novels from the memory of an ideal past to the anticipation of an ideal future. In between, the present is the valley of the shadow, the darkness just before the dawn. The novels are driven by the expectation that things will have to get much worse before they can get any better – but that these better times will inevitably come.

This book has been written with the same hope – that long-term decline will be followed by the glory of a better world – but this book does not share the novels' expectation that the immediate future is to be one of inevitable and inescapable gloom. It is possible that true believers and faithful churches will pursue a path of constant reformation even as the world and the professing church inevitably decay (as is suggested in the 'kingdom parables' of Matthew 13). The past does often appear to have been better – at least in the moments when the church was at its best – and the church's future is certainly glorious. But evangelicals do not need to regard the present world as something that must be endured or escaped. There is work to be done – and the returning King instructs us to 'occupy till I come' (Luke 19:13).

Our duties, as we wait for the Lord from heaven, include the constant pursuit of the reformation of the church, its doctrine and practice, and the constant pursuit of increasing purity in the Christian life. This book has been written with a concern that the *Left Behind* series, and associated rapture fictions, might actually stand in the way of that task. While the novels contain much that should be commended, they are popularising some of the most disturbing and even dangerous trends in contemporary evangelicalism. The recent spate of rapture novels is a reflection of the modern evangelical crisis. 'How far would God let this go before sending the conquering King?'[3]

ESCHATOLOGY AND THE GOSPEL

This pursuit of constant reformation does not require us to abandon the novels' constant hope for the Lord's return. In fact, every aspect of the reformation that modern evangelicalism needs is directly related to the 'blessed hope'.

The doctrines that would be involved in the reformation of evangelicalism can be analysed in the familiar terms of the 'now' and the 'not yet'. That tension between what we now have and what we will have, what we now are and what we will become, is nowhere more obvious than in the New Testament teaching concerning the experience of salvation. The terminology of salvation redounds with future hope: those who trust in Jesus Christ are given 'eternal life', spiritual life that can never end; they are 'justified', knowing in the present the unchanging verdict of the Final Judgement; and they are 'sanctified', made 'saints', set apart for God's presence and service, even as they are being made holy (Heb. 10:14). This is the reason why those who are justified by faith can have 'peace with God' (Rom. 5:1) – the believer's present knowledge of the acquittal of the Final Judgement cannot be overturned. The saints in heaven are happier than we are – but, in terms of their future, they cannot be any more secure than we are. What we have 'now' anticipates in a real way what we will enjoy in the 'not yet'.

ESCHATOLOGY AND THE CHURCH

It is this confidence that should mark the gatherings together of the Lord's people. Our churches are fellowships of 'saints', churches of people who have, in an important sense, already entered into the life of heaven (Col. 3:1-4). We are heaven's citizens, and our congregations are outposts of the kingdom (Phil. 3:20). The 'now' is a very real anticipation of the 'not yet'.

That fellowship with heaven should be marked in our worship. When we worship, we already 'come unto mount Sion, and unto the city of the living God, the heavenly Jerusalem, and to an innumerable company of angels, to the general assembly and church of the firstborn, which are written in heaven, and to God the Judge of all, and to the spirits of just men made perfect, and to Jesus the mediator of the new covenant, and to the blood of sprinkling, that speaketh better things than that of Abel' (Heb. 12:22-24). This is what 'going to church' is really all about. Our fellowship with heaven should influence our use of the ordinances – baptism, the symbol of entering a life as unending as that of the risen Lord Jesus (Rom. 6:4), and the Lord's Supper, the memorial feast we continue until he comes (1 Cor. 11:26) as we anticipate the great 'marriage supper of the Lamb' (Rev. 19:7-9). Every right administration of the Lord's Supper should include a look back, to Calvary, a look up, towards Christ in heavenly glory, and a look forward, to that grandest of all reunions, when we shall see him as he is. Grace, as Archbishop James Ussher put it, is but glory in the bud: what we have 'now' anticipates what we will enjoy in the 'not yet'.

ESCHATOLOGY AND THE CHRISTIAN LIFE

But there is tension amidst the glory. Every Christian is a war zone, in which the forces of the old and new worlds battle for territorial control. The perpetual conflict is described in passages like Galatians 5:17-18, the 'now' which goes on to speak of the virtues created by the Spirit in those who are being prepared as heirs of the future kingdom. There is tension, too, as the Christian lives in the world. Jesus' 'high priestly prayer' describes the world's constant opposition to the values of Jesus Christ, even as it indicates the glory of the future, when the believer is finally taken from the world and is allowed a sight of what cannot now be seen (John 17:24). But there is also tension in the world, in the fabric of the created order as it suffers the consequences of the fall and anticipates the glory of its redemption. The Christian's relationship with himself is paralleled by the Christian's relationship to the history of creation, 'made subject to vanity, not willingly, but by reason of him who subjected the same in hope' until it is 'delivered from the bondage of corruption into the glorious liberty of the children of God' (Rom. 8:20-21). Like the world in which he lives, the Christian is a site of conflict, so that 'we who have the firstfruits of the Spirit ... groan within ourselves, waiting for the adoption ... the redemption of the body' (Rom. 8:23). But the tension of the present will disappear. The cosmos will be renewed when the glory of God shines out from the people of God: 'the earnest expectation of the [creation] waiteth for the manifestation of the sons of God' (Rom. 8:19). This tension amidst the glory is the present reality for God's people. John explains that it is not obvious to us what we shall be (1 John 3:2), but neither is it obvious to the world what we already are. The frustrations of the 'now' will certainly give way to the realisation of what is still 'not yet'.

So the fallen world will one day be renewed. In the meantime, Christians should be busy, for the fallen world is the sphere of our activity. We are to be builders, 'occupying' ourselves with kingdom works of evangelism and service. Every Christian has a strong incentive for action. Although we are saved by grace, we will be judged by works (1 Cor. 3:13-15), 'rewarded' for works that are the fruit of grace in our lives. The 'now' is a time of preparation for the 'not yet'. We are to be constantly ready, for our works will be evaluated when Jesus Christ returns. And that readiness doesn't only imply activity – it also requires 'abiding'. John sums it up well when he encourages us to 'abide in him; that, when he shall appear, we may have confidence, and not be ashamed before him at his coming' (1 John 2:28). That fact that so many translations prefer 'if' to 'when' highlights an important variation in the Greek textual traditions, but the variation adds to the significance of the statement. Both variations are necessary – 'when', the ultimate certainty that Jesus Christ is returning, and 'if', the constant possibility that he could return more rapidly than we imagine. At any moment, the 'now' could be interrupted by the 'not yet'.

God's people have long waited for the realisation of his promises. One hundred and fifty years ago, Bishop J. C. Ryle wrote of our constant hope:

> Yet a little while, and the last sermon will be preached, the last congregation shall break up. … Live as if you thought Christ might come at any time. Do everything as if you did it for the last time. Say everything as if you said it for the last time. Read every chapter in the Bible as if you did not know whether you would be allowed to read it again. Pray every prayer as if you felt it might be your last opportunity. Hear every sermon as if you were hearing it once and for ever. This is the way to be found ready.[4]

As Ryle explains it, the challenge to every Christian is to evaluate life choices in the present as we will when we finally stand before God.

GOING HOME

Every Christian is going home. At times, the way seems long and the circumstances of travel discouraging. The present is bleak, and the future promises no better. Yet Romans 8:38-39 assures us that even 'things to come' shall not 'be able to separate us from the love of God, which is in Christ Jesus our Lord'. We are going home; 'yet a little while, and he that shall come will come, and will not tarry' (Heb. 10:37).

We must not lose that perspective. The call to pursue the reformation of evangelicalism is not one that requires us to abandon the 'blessed hope' – but rather one that requires us to live in its constant expectation, to work from it towards the renewal of the church. True eschatology is not the ally of doctrinal minimalism. Biblical eschatology has a bearing on every theological issue, whether conversion, church fellowship, or the Christian life. We do not need to choose between our expectation of the second coming and our great hopes for reformation in the church.

Evangelicalism is in crisis; but the doctrine of the Second Coming, better understood, is not a cause of the current malaise. Jesus Christ is returning, and he will not be disappointed. In the midst of the darkness of ecclesiastical decay, the returning merchant discovers a 'pearl of great price', which he sells everything to posses (Matt. 13:45-46). The pearl is the church; the merchant the Saviour; and the call for reformation is clear. For some, at least, there will be an escape from the dangers of the evangelical crisis.

APPENDIX

THIS VOLUME HAS BEEN WRITTEN to highlight the opportunities and dangers represented by the rapture fiction phenomenon. As we have seen, the sale of tens of millions of copies of *Left Behind* has created an environment, at least in the USA, where more people are reading and thinking about the return of Jesus Christ than, perhaps, ever before. At the same time, this volume has argued that the series' presentation of the Christian faith is not without its dangers – we have noticed that a growing number of evangelicals, including a number of dispensationalists, have been voicing their concerns.

It is possible that many people reading this book have themselves come from a dispensational background, or are thinking through the claims made by some of the movement's leaders. It may be that, having read something of the problems of the rapture fiction phenomenon, and wondering whether these problems are to some extent rooted in dispensationalism itself, these readers would be interested in examining alternatives with equally evangelical credentials. The purpose of this appendix is to demonstrate that such alternative systems of theology do exist, and that those who are concerned by the rapture fiction phenomenon or certain aspects of the dispensational movement might want to consider their claims.

NO ALTERNATIVE TO DISPENSATIONS

Of course, to suggest that we should reconsider dispensationalism is not to suggest that we should read the Bible without any concern for dispensational differences. Evangelicals, tracing the biblical development of the plan of salvation, have to believe in dispensations. Emphasising the finality of the atonement provided in Christ's death, no evangelical could encourage anyone to revert to the system of sacrifices that Old Testament believers used. The argument of Hebrews, therefore, is that the work of Jesus Christ has brought to an end the redemptive value of Jewish ceremony and liturgy. Paul argues time and again that those who revert to the patterns of worship that formerly prevailed are in effect denying the value of the work of Jesus Christ. Evangelicals need dispensations if they are to accurately trace the flow of redemptive history, and thereby understand the gospel.

Classical Protestant, Reformed and evangelical thinking – including classical dispensationalism – has always reflected this. The most important of the seventeenth-century English confessions of faith, for example, insists on the necessity of distinguishing the dispensations. The Westminster Confession of Faith (1647) argues strongly that the plan of God is one in all ages, and that an unchanging covenant of grace extends from the gates of Eden to the gates of the New Jerusalem. Instead of seeing seven or more differentiated periods in redemptive history, each with a distinctive set of demands for the believer, it argues that God's gracious covenant purposes unite the people of God in both Old and New Testament ages. It recognises that differences between these ages do exist, but 'there are not therefore two covenants of grace, differing in substance, but one and the same, under various dispensations' (WCF 7:6).

This sensitivity to dispensational differences has been reflected in the writings of many of the most significant of Protestant and evangelical thinkers. There have been differences in the approaches and conclusions of those evangelical writers who have considered the discontinuities of Scripture. Nevertheless, evangelical leaders have been right to insist on the necessity of recognising dispensational distinctions. Reading the Bible without any awareness of dispensational distinctions obscures the redemptive-historical changes brought about by the life and work of Jesus Christ. According to Paul, and the writer of the letter to the Hebrews, a failure to understand the implications of these changes threatens the nature of the gospel itself.

MANY ALTERNATIVES TO DISPENSATIONALISM

Nevertheless, while there is no alternative to our recognising the existence of redemptive-historical dispensations, there are many alternatives to the system of dispensationalism outlined by Darby and provided with a classic twentieth-century expression in the *Scofield Reference Bible* (1909; second edition 1917). We have already noticed that 'popular' dispensationalism – a simplified and colourful variety that has been most famously expounded in books like Hal Lindsey's *The Late Great Planet Earth* (1970) – differs significantly from the more careful and reliable statements of the best theologians in the movement. Classical dispensational writing moved in two directions throughout the twentieth century: on the one hand, popular dispensationalism and rapture fiction writing weakened its wider interest in theology and made it more appealing to larger audiences; on the other hand, academic dispensationalists developed many of the movement's central ideas and demanded that its conclusions should be reconsidered and sometimes even overturned.

REVISED DISPENSATIONALISM

One of the most obvious examples of the latter trend was the publication of the *New Scofield Reference Bible* in 1967. This revision of

Scofield's text clarified the extent to which dispensational thinking had developed through the fifty years since the publication of his influential second edition in 1917. We have already noted that two leading Reformed theologians, A. A. Hoekema and O. Palmer Robertson, expressed their appreciation for the clarification of dispensational theology this volume represented: Hoekema appreciatively summarised the notes as teaching that 'in each dispensation there is only one basis for salvation: by God's grace through the work of Christ accomplished on the cross and vindicated in his resurrection.'[1]

These revisions were similarly valued among many of those who had expressed concern at some of the movement's earlier conclusions. Nevertheless, this insistence on a single way of salvation was balanced by a continuing commitment to the 'two peoples of God' theory. Although they would gain salvation on the same basis, the earthly status and spiritual future of Israel and the church were still carefully distinguished. Classical dispensationalism had changed its emphases, but its central themes remained the same.

PROGRESSIVE DISPENSATIONALISM

This interest in the revision of dispensationalism accelerated towards the end of the twentieth century. Craig A. Blaising and Darrell L. Bock were both professors at Dallas Theological Seminary when they published their ground-breaking study of *Progressive Dispensationalism* (1993).[2] Their workplace alone made their initiative controversial, for, throughout the twentieth century, Dallas Seminary had been a flagship institution of the classical dispensational movement. It had been founded by L. S. Chafer after an extensive correspondence with J. Gresham Machen, founder of Westminster Theological Seminary. Machen had hoped that both institutions would help stem the early twentieth-century drift towards theological modernism by constructing a confessional Presbyterian alternative, but Chafer set Dallas on a different course and developed his moderate Calvinism alongside distinctly dispensational themes in a twelve-volume systematic theology. The fact that the authors of *Progressive Dispensationalism* were two Dallas scholars therefore generated fears among many classical dispensationalists that the key themes of their system were being abandoned in the very centre where the most able of its modern exponents had been trained.

There was certainly good reason for their concern. Perhaps the most significant difference between classical and progressive dispensationalism is that the latter denies the movement's earlier distinction between Israel and the church. The importance of this development should not be under-estimated – especially when it is remembered that Chafer's earlier definition of the system had placed this distinction at its heart. There can be little doubt that *Progressive Dispensationalism* has demonstrated that some of the movement's most important thinkers are prepared to radically re-think their understanding of redemptive history. It remains to be seen how widely their revisions will be adopted, what impact they will have on dispensational thinking about the end, and to what extent this progressive dispensationalism will attract the sympathy and support of covenant theologians.

NEW COVENANT THEOLOGY

New Covenant Theology sits somewhere between the various systems of dispensationalism and their covenant theology cousins. Like the various forms of dispensationalism, New Covenant Theology claims that the Old and New Testaments are totally separate. Unlike traditional forms of Reformed covenant theology, it claims that the New Testament believer is not under any law except the 'law of Christ', which, as its name suggests, is contained in the New Covenant. As the New Covenant repeats nine of the Ten Commandments, therefore, discussions about the validity of New Covenant Theology often centre on the issue of the Sabbath. New Covenant theologians, including D. A. Carson and John Piper, have often emerged from conservative Reformed backgrounds, and their writing has invested their system with considerable appeal.[3] Some of those who adopt this perspective refer, for theological support, to the confession of faith produced by London Baptists in 1644.

Reformed Baptist covenant theology

But the mainstream of Reformed Baptist theology changed quite quickly through the seventeenth century and, in 1677 and again in 1689, English Baptist leaders signed another confession of faith that re-stated the central themes of the wider Reformed tradition. The approach encapsulated in their 1689 Confession shares many of the interests of New Covenant Theology, but argues for the essential similarity of all covenants since the promises given to Adam and Eve in Genesis 3. Every covenant since Genesis 3, in other words, has been the expression of an underlying covenant of grace which unites all of the biblical covenants to make the same promise: 'I will be your God'. This version of Reformed Baptist theology differs from New Covenant Theology in that it sees the critical discontinuity between the dispensations in Genesis 3, rather than between the Old and New Testaments. The major contrast in Reformed Baptist theology is between the covenant of works and the covenant of grace, not between the Mosaic administration and the new covenant introduced by the work of Christ, which it regards as different dispensations within the covenant of grace.

Reformed covenant theology, in general, argues that God dealt with humanity before the fall by means of a covenant of works. This covenant of works was premised on obedience. Adam and Eve had to fulfil certain conditions if they were to enjoy the eternal life that God was offering to them. They failed to obey, but their failure did not lead God to reject them. Instead, he initiated a new covenant, the covenant of grace, in which his promises to his people were conditional – not on their works, but on the faith and repentance he provided. The terms of this covenant of grace were implicit until they were detailed in God's dealings with Abraham (Gen. 15-17), which summarised its terms under a three-fold promise to provide Abraham and his believing descendants with a seed, a blessing, and a land. In the Old Testament, these promises had a physical as well as a spiritual fulfilment, in that believing Israelites marked their male seed with the covenant sign of circumcision, enjoyed the blessings for obedience outlined in passages like Deuteronomy 28, and, while faithful, enjoyed life in the promised land. But Reformed Baptist theology, perhaps most ably in Paul K. Jewett's *Infant Baptism and the Covenant of*

Grace (1978), argues that these promises have another application in the New Testament. Those who share Abraham's faith have been provided with the ultimate seed, Jesus Christ (Gal. 3:29); the ultimate blessings, forgiveness of sins and the filling of the Holy Spirit (Rom. 4:9; Gal. 3:16); and the ultimate land, the new heavens and the new earth (Rom. 4:13-17; Heb. 11:16). Christians, as Abraham's spiritual descendents, have become the heirs of the world – and heirs of heaven – through faith. But our status in the new covenant does not do away with our responsibilities to the other covenants, for New Covenant believers are still under the terms of the moral law (Rom. 13:9).

REFORMED 'PAEDOBAPTIST' COVENANT THEOLOGY

The covenant theology adopted by many of the other Puritan groups shared the basic premises of the 1689 Confession, but also argued that the terms of the new covenant did not exclude the children of believers, who, throughout the Old Testament dispensations of the covenant of grace, had always been regarded as covenant members. Noticing that each of the Old Testament covenants were made to covenant mediators and all those they represented – most famously, to Abraham and his 'seed' – they argued that the infants of believers should be understood as being 'in covenant' with God and should therefore take the mark of covenant membership. Thus was laid the theological foundation for infant baptism, which has also become known as 'paedobaptism'.

Of all the alternatives to dispensationalism, this traditional paedobaptist covenant theology probably offers the widest literature. Perhaps the most helpful discussions of this position would be O. Palmer Robertson's *The Christ of the Covenants* (1980), and David McKay's *The Bond of Love* (2001), both of which also offer a useful comparison between paedobaptist covenant theology and dispensationalism.

THE NATURE OF THEOLOGICAL DEBATE

Lamentably, the debate between dispensational theologians and their various opponents has not always been characterised by the grace that is at the heart of the dispute. It does not take long for someone reading into the differences between these approaches to find uncharitable assertions and statements that might even be construed as the bearing of false witness. It would be very easy for a concerned Christian to look at the language of the debate and conclude that the discussion has a more obvious relation to the purposes of evil than the gracious pursuit of truth.

But if the debate often generates more heat than light, it also indicates how serious are the issues at stake. Of course, there are plenty of red herrings – deciding who really adopts a 'literal hermeneutic' (and no one does so consistently) is probably less important than deciding the place of the law in the believer's life. Nevertheless, the unedifying spectacle of Christians in disagreement is not an excuse for the believer's decision to ignore these important theological issues. As rapture novels increase in public influence, believers will have many opportunities to speak out, and it is important that they are properly prepared.

PRE-MILLENNIALISM NOT PRECLUDED

As the above survey demonstrates, therefore, there are a number of alternatives to dispensationalism. Each of these alternatives are credibly evangelical, upholding the infallibility and uniqueness of Scripture and, their respective advocates would maintain, pointing to the glory of God in creation and redemption. It is also important to note that none of these alternatives automatically precludes pre-millennialism, although most would certainly find the idea of the pre-tribulation rapture problematic. Someone moving from dispensationalism towards any one of the alternatives this appendix has listed would therefore be able to find advocates of their new position who hold to firmly pre-millennial expectations. But that is not to say that any of these alternatives to dispensationalism is inherently pre-millennial, either; just as these alternatives do not preclude pre-millennialism, neither do they preclude other forms of millennial belief.

FURTHER READING

RAPTURE NOVELS DISCUSSED IN THIS BOOK

Sidney Watson, *Scarlet and Purple* (1913), *The Mark of the Beast* (1915), and *In the Twinkling of an Eye* (1916)

Salem Kirban, *666* (1970) and *1000* (1973)

The 'Left Behind' series, co-authored by Tim LaHaye and Jerry B. Jenkins, and published by Tyndale:

> *Left Behind* (1995)
> *Tribulation Force* (1996)
> *Nicolae* (1997)

Soul Harvest (1998)
Apollyon (1999)
Assassins (1999)
The Indwelling (2000)
The Mark (2000)
Desecration (2001)
The Remnant (2002)
Armageddon (2003)
The Glorious Appearing (2004)

Prequel: *The Rising* (2005)
Sequel: Still to be published.

The series website can be found at www.leftbehind.com.

RAPTURE NOVELS PUBLISHED BY TYNDALE THAT CAPITALISE ON LEFT BEHIND

Med Odom, *Apocalypse Dawn* (2003), *Apocalypse Burning* (2004), *Apocalypse Crucible* (2004)

Neesa Hart, *End of State* (2004), *Impeachable Offense* (2004), *Necessary Evils* (2005)

RAPTURE NOVELS PUBLISHED BY OTHER PUBLISHING HOUSES THST CAPITALISE ON LEFT BEHIND

Jerry B. Jenkins, *Soon* (2003), *Silenced* (2004)
Tim LaHaye and Greg Dinallo, *Bablyon Rising* (2004)
Tim LaHaye and Bob Phillips, *The Secret on Ararat* (2004)

SELECT BIBLIOGRAPHY

Paul Boyer, *When Time Shall Be No More: Prophecy Belief in Modern American Culture* (Cambridge, MA: The Belknap Press of Harvard University Press, 1992)
Bruce David Forbes and Jeanne Halgren Kilde (eds), *Rapture, Revelation and the End Times: Exploring the Left Behind Series* (New

York: Palgrave Macmillan, 2004)

Amy Johnson Frykholm, *Rapture Culture: Left Behind in Evangelical America* (Oxford: Oxford University Press, 2004)

Reginald C. Kimbro, *The Gospel according to Dispensationalism* (Toronto: Wittenberg Publications, 1995)

Glenn W. Shuck, *Marks of the Beast: The Left Behind Novels and the Struggle for Evangelical Identity* (New York: New York University Press, 2005)

Michael Williams, *This World is Not My Home: The Origins and Development Of Dispensationalism* (Fearn, Ross-shire: Mentor, 2003)

Dwight Wilson, *Armageddon Now! The Premillenarian Response to Russia and Israel Since 1917* (1977; reprinted Tyler, TX: Institute for Christian Economics, 1991)

NOTES

PREFACE

1. The evangelical crisis has been described in David F. Wells, *No Place for Truth: or Whatever Happened to Evangelical Theology* (Grand Rapids, Michigan: Eerdmans, 1996), and Os Guinness, *Fit Bodies, Fat Minds: Why Evangelicals Don't Think and What to Do About It* (Grand Rapids, Michigan: Baker, 1994).

2. There is a suggestion that Boice abandoned the dispensationalism of *The Last and Future World* (Grand Rapids, Michigan: Zondervan, 1974), while retaining his wider commitment to pre-millennialism. Despite his published attacks on some of the implications of the system, especially in relation to the 'Lordship salvation' debate, MacArthur appears to have retained a broadly dispensational and pre-millennial worldview.

CHAPTER I

1. *Tribulation Force* (1996), p. 352. Full bibliographical details of all novels cited in the footnotes can be found in the section on 'Further reading'.

2. The official *Left Behind* website can be found on www.leftbehind.com. Unofficial fan websites include www.tribforcehq.com.

3. Sales figures for *The Lord of the Rings* are available on www.theonering.net/perl/newsview/2/995143527, accessed 12 December 2005.

4. Bernard McGinn (general ed.), *The Encyclopedia of Apocalypticism* (New York: Continuum, 1998), 3 volumes; Norman Cohn, *The Pursuit of the Millennium: Revolutionary Millenarians and Mystical Anarchists of the Middle Ages* (1957; rpt. London: Mercury Books, 1962).

5. Norman Cohn, *Cosmos, Chaos and The World to Come: The Ancient Roots of Apocalyptic Faith* (London: Yale University Press, 1993).

6. The millennial thinking of Communists and Nazis was documented in Cohn, *The Pursuit of the Millennium*.

7. 'How the Year 2000 bug will hurt the economy', *Business Week* 2 March 1998, pp. 46-51; 'Bank boss fears global crash in 2000', *Sunday Times: Money* 29 March 1998, p. 1.

8. David Rice, 'Taking the apocalyptic pulse of Muslims in Israel and Egypt', www.mille.org/stew/fall99/cook-fall99.html, accessed January 2005. This paper is hosted on the website of the Centre for Millennial Studies, Boston University, Boston, MA.

9. David Rice, 'Islam and apocalyptic', www.mille.org/scholarship/papers/cookabs.html, accessed December 2004. This paper is hosted on the website of the Centre for Millennial Studies, Boston University, Boston, MA.

10. Subsequently, the *Daily Telegraph* has reported that members of the Iraqi resistance to American occupation believed they were witnessing the fulfilment of a centuries-old Shia prophecy: 'One day, Iraq will be taken over by white foreigners. There will be poor people who fight them and they will fight until Basra burns. Then the al-Mahdi will appear with Jesus and the 12 prophets to liberate

the world'; 'Besieged Shias fear the prophecy of Armageddon', *Daily Telegraph* 14 August 2004, p. 4.

11. 'Tax numbers spark devil of a row in Church', *Daily Telegraph* 20 February 2001, p. 19.

12. See, for example, Gary North, *The Sinai Strategy: Economics and the Ten Commandments* (Tyler, TX: Institute for Christian Economics, 1986), pp. 87-90.

13. Charles M. Sennott, 'Jerusalem on high alert as 2000 nears', *Boston Globe* 14 December 1999, http://www.rickross.com/reference/millenium/millenium56.html, accessed December 2004.

14. The FBI report, 'Project Megiddo', has been published alongside Israeli security reports in Jeffrey Kaplan (ed.), *Millennial Violence: Past, Present and Future* (London: Frank Cass, 2002).

15. Francis Fukuyama, *The End of History and the Last Man* (London: Penguin, 1993); Samuel P. Huntingdon, *The Clash of Civilisations and the Remaking of World Order* (London: Free Press, 2002).

16. Robert Kagan, *Paradise & Power: America and Europe in the New World Order* (London: Atlantic Books, 2003), p. 73.

17. See, for example, 'Tribulations', *Times Literary Supplement* 4 February 2005, p. 9.

18. Readers will find a balanced exposition of dispensationalism in Dwight Pentecost, *Things to Come: A Study in Biblical Eschatology* (Grand Rapids, MI: Zondervan, 1958).

19. Mark Hitchcock, *Is the Antichrist Alive Today?* (Sisters, Oregon: Multnomah, 2002).

20. Philip Jenkins, *Mystics and Messiahs: Cults and New Religions in American History* (Oxford: Oxford University Press, 2000), p. 5.

21. Dwight Wilson, *Armageddon Now! The Premillenarian Response to Russia and Israel since 1917* (Grand Rapids: Baker, 1977), p. 12.

22. Stephen Sizer, *Christian Zionism: Road-map to Armageddon?* (Leicester: IVP, 2004), p. 23.

23. Paul Boyer, *When Time Shall Be No More: Prophecy Belief in Modern American Culture* (Cambridge, MA: Belknap Press, 1992), p. 141; George M. Marsden, 'Fundamentalism as an American Phenomenon', in D. G. Hart (ed.), *Reckoning with the Past* (Grand

Rapids: Baker, 1995), p. 319; James Mills, 'The serious implications of a 1971 conversation with Ronald Reagan: A footnote to current history', *San Diego Magazine* (August 1985), p. 141, quoted in Boyer, *When Time Shall be No More* (1992), p. 142; Sizer, *Christian Zionism: Road-map to Armageddon?* (2004), pp. 86-89.

24. Ronald Reagan, 'Address to the National Association of Evangelicals, March 8, 1983', in Paul Boyer (ed.), *Reagan as President: Contemporary Views of the Man, His Politics, and His Policies* (Chicago: Ivan R. Dee, 1990), pp. 165-69.

25. Sizer, *Christian Zionism: Road-map to Armageddon?* (2004), p. 105.

26. 'The end of the world: A brief history', *The Economist* 18 December 2004, p. 79.

27. *Time*, 1 July 2002, and *Newsweek*, 24 May 2004.

28. http://www.carl-olson.com/rapture_articles.html; http://www.diocese-gal-hou.org/youngacm/left_behind.htm

29. Amy Johnson Frykholm, *Rapture Culture:* Left Behind *in Evangelical America* (Oxford: OUP, 2004), p. 89.

30. Melani McAlister, 'Prophecy, politics and the popular: the *Left Behind* series and Christian fundamentalism's New World Order', *South Atlantic Quarterly* 102:4 (2003), p. 782.

31. Frykholm, *Rapture Culture* (2004), p. 178.

32. Frykholm, *Rapture Culture* (2004), p. 89.

33. Anne Lamott, 'Knocking on heaven's door', *Travelling Mercies: Some Thoughts on Faith* (New York: Pantheon, 1999), p. 60, quoted in Frykholm, *Rapture Culture* (2004), p. 177.

34. See, for example, 'Beam me up Jesus', aired as part of Channel 4's 'Putting the fun in fundamental' series in autumn 2004 on UK television; http://www.chanel4.com/culture/microsites/B/believeitomot/debates/fundamental1.html.

35. Richard Morrison, 'Armageddon ahead, please fasten your Bible belt', *The Times* T2, 20 September 2002, pp. 2-3.

36. George Baxter Pfoertner, 'The Profits of Doom', *The Independent on Sunday* magazine supplement, 12 November 2000, p. 10. There might be some evidence for that in such statements as "the night was as black as Carpathia's soul"; *Nicolae* (1997), p. 109.

37. Christopher Tayler, 'Rapt attention', *Times Literary Supplement*, 7 May 2004, p. 36. The original twelve volumes are to be followed by two prequels and a sequel.

38. Tayler, 'Rapt attention' (2004), p. 36.

39. Steve Wohlberg, *The Left Behind Deception: Revealing Dangerous Errors about the Rapture and the Antichrist* (Coldwater, MI: Remnant Publications, 2001). Additional information can be found on www.truthleftbehind.com.

40. A number of Roman Catholic authors who have published attacks on the series are themselves former dispensationalists. See, for example, Carl E. Olson, *Will Catholics be "Left Behind"?* (Ft Collins, CO: Ignatius Press, 2003).

41. Gary DeMar, *End Times Fiction: A Biblical Consideration of the Left Behind Theology* (Nashville, TN: Thomas Nelson, 2001).

42. Daniel Hertzler, 'Assessing the "Left Behind" Phenomenon', in Loren L. Johns (ed.), *Apocalypticism and Millennialism: Shaping a Believers Church Eschatology for the Twenty-First Century* (Kitchener, Ont: Pandora Press, 2000), p. 363.

43. Lisa Ruby, *God's Wrath on Left Behind* (North Attleboro, MA: Liberty to the Captives Publications, 2002).

44. Nathan D. Wilson, *Right Behind: A Parody of Last Days Goofiness* (Moscow, ID: Canon Press, 2001), p. 9.

45. This is an interpretive approach to Revelation that is called 'preterism'. Preterist ideas have been advanced in a number of recent publications, including R. C. Sproul, *The Last Days According to Jesus: When did Jesus say he would return?* (Grand Rapids, Michigan: Baker, 1998).

46. See comments by Stephen Spencer, formerly professor of theology at Dallas Theological Seminary, as quoted in Mark Reasoner, 'What does the Bible say about the end times? A Biblical studies discussion of interpretive methods', in Bruce David Forbes and Jeanne Halgren Kilde (eds), *Rapture, Revelation and the End Times: Exploring the Left Behind Series* (New York: Palgrave Macmillan, 2004), p. 90.

47. Mark Sweetnam makes this point in his essay in Kenneth G. C. Newport and Crawford Gribben (eds), *Expectations of the End: Contemporary Millennialism in Social and Historical Context* (Baylor,

TX: Baylor University Press, 2006).

48. Bruce David Forbes, 'How popular are the Left Behind books ... and why?', in Bruce David Forbes and Jeanne Halgren Kilde (eds), *Rapture, Revelation and the End Times: Exploring the Left Behind Series* (New York: Palgrave Macmillan, 2004), p. 9.

CHAPTER 2

1. *Tribulation Force* (1996), pp. 66-67.

2. *Nicolae* (1997), pp. 45-46.

3. *The Remnant* (2002), p. 210.

4. Gary L. Nebeker, 'John Nelson Darby and Trinity College, Dublin: A study in eschatological contrasts', *Fides et Historia* 34 (2002), pp. 87-108.

5. Brethren would reject the 'Plymouth' label as unnecessarily denominational, but I have retained it here to distinguish these Brethren from others bearing similar names.

6. [J. N. Darby], *Letters of J.N.D.*, ed. William Kelly (London: Stow Hill Bible and Tract Depot, n.d.), ii. 254.

7. The following paragraphs are heavily dependent on Timothy C. F. Stunt, 'Influences in the early life of J. N. Darby', in Crawford Gribben and Timothy C. F. Stunt (eds), *Prisoners of Hope? Aspects of Evangelical Millennialism in Britain and Ireland, 1800-1880* (Carlisle: Paternoster, 2004), pp. 50-52.

8. Timothy Larsen (general ed.), *Biographical Dictionary of Evangelicals* (Leicester: IVP, 2003), s.v.

9. [Darby], *Letters of J.N.D.* (n.d.), iii. 297.

10. [Darby], *Letters of J.N.D.* (n.d.), iii. 297.

11. Quoted in F. Roy Coad, *A History of the Brethren Movement* (Exeter: Paternoster, 1968), pp. 25-26.

12. [Darby], *Letters of J.N.D.* (n.d.), iii. 297.

13. [Darby], *Letters of J.N.D.* (n.d.), iii. 453-4

14. J. N. Darby, *Collected Writings* (Winschoten, Netherlands: H. L. Heijkoop, 1972), xviii. 146, 156.

15. Darby, *Collected Writings* (1972), xviii. 156.

16. See, in addition to MacPherson's published documents, the resources maintained on http://www.preteristarchive.com/

PartialPreterism/macpherson-dave_dd_01.html, accessed January 2005. See also Thomas Ice, 'Why the doctrine of the pretribulational rapture did not begin with Margaret Macdonald,' *Bibliotheca Sacra* 147 (1990), pp. 155-68.

17. http://www.preteristarchive.com/dEmEnTia/tarkowski-ed_dd_01.html, accessed January 2005.

18. Stunt, 'Influences in the early life of J. N. Darby' (2004).

19. Stunt, 'Influences in the early life of J. N. Darby' (2004).

20. S. P. Tregelles to B. W. Newton, 29 January 1857, Christian Brethren Archive, John Rylands University Library, Manchester, 7181 (7).

21. A more detailed treatment of this subject can be found in E. R. Sandeen, *The Roots of Fundamentalism: British and American Millenarianism, 1800-1930* (Chicago: University of Chicago Press, 1970).

22. The only modern biography is Joseph M. Canfield, *The Incredible Scofield and his Book* (Vallecito, California: Ross House Books, 1988). Canfield's biography is academically weak.

23. Darby, *Collected Writings* (1972), xiv. 40.

24. Darby, *Collected Writings* (1972), i. 351.

25. Peter S. Ruckman, *Millions Disappear! Fact or Fiction?* (Pensacola, Florida: Bible Baptist Bookstore, n.d.)

26. C. C. Ryrie, *Dispensationalism Today* (Chicago: Moody Press, 1965), p. 179.

27. Ryrie, *Dispensationalism Today* (1965), p. 183.

28. Ryrie, *Dispensationalism Today* (1965), p. 190.

29. Ryrie, *Dispensationalism Today* (1965), pp. 190-191.

30. Robert L. Reymond, *A New Systematic Theology of the Christian Faith* (Nashville, Tennessee: Thomas Nelson, 1998), p. 507.

31. Reymond, *A New Systematic Theology* (1998), p. 509.

32. C.C. Ryrie, 'Dispensationalism', in Walter A. Elwell (ed.), *Evangelical Dictionary of Theology* (London: Marshall Pickering, 1984), pp. 321-323.

33. A.A. Hoekema, *The Bible and the Future* (Grand Rapids: Eerdmans, 1979), p. 195.

34. O. Palmer Robertson, *The Christ of the Covenants*

(Phillipsburg, New Jersey: Presbyterian and Reformed, 1980), p. 216.

35. Mark Noll, *The Scandal of the Evangelical Mind* (Leicester: IVP, 1994), pp. 117f.; Alister McGrath, *Evangelicalism and the Future of Christianity* (London: Hodder and Stoughton, 1994), p. 21; Os Guinness, *Fit Bodies, Fat Minds: Why evangelicals don't think and what to do about it* (London: Hodder and Stoughton, 1995), pp. 66f. By contrast, Iain H. Murray's *Evangelicalism Divided: A Record of Crucial Change in the years 1950 to 2000* (Edinburgh: Banner of Truth, 2000) pins the blame for evangelical decay on Noll and McGrath's challenge to Biblical inerrancy.

36. *Tribulation Force* (1996), p. 67.

CHAPTER 3

1. *Left Behind* (1995), pp. 79-80.

2. Timothy Larsen (general ed.), *Biographical Dictionary of Evangelicals* (Leicester: IVP, 2003), s.v.

3. Hal Lindsey, *There's a New World Coming* (Eugene, Oregon: Harvest House, 1973; updated 1984), p. 8; *The Apocalypse Code* (Palos Verdes, CA: Western Front, 1997), p. 36; Lindsey, *The Apocalypse Code* (1997), pp. 42, 72.

4. Stephen Sizer, *Christian Zionism: Road-map to Armageddon?* (Leicester: IVP, 2004), p. 214; George M. Marsden, 'Fundamentalism as an American Phenomenon', in D.G. Hart (ed.), *Reckoning with the Past* (Grand Rapids: Baker, 1995), 319; Paul Boyer, *When Time Shall Be No More: Prophecy Belief in Modern American Culture* (Cambridge: Belknap Press, 1992), *passim*.

5. Amy Johnson Frykholm, *Rapture Culture: Left Behind in Evangelical America* (Oxford: OUP, 2004), pp. 205-207.

6. *Scarlet and Purple: A Story of Souls and 'Signs'* (London: William Nicholson & Sons, [1913]; rpr. Edinburgh: B. McCall Barbour, 1974); *The Mark of the Beast* (London: W. Nicholson & Sons, [1915]; rpr. Edinburgh: B. McCall Barbour, 1974); *In the Twinkling of an Eye* (London: W. Nicholson & Sons, [1916]).

7. *Scarlet and Purple* (1913; 1974), p. 160.

8. *In the Twinkling of an Eye* (1916), p. vi.

9. *The Mark of the Beast* (1915; 1974), p. 5.

10. *In the Twinkling of an Eye* (1916), p. vi-vii.

11. *In the Twinkling of an Eye* (1916), p.12.

12. *In the Twinkling of an Eye* (1916), p. 46.

13. *In the Twinkling of an Eye* (1916), p. 43.

14. *In the Twinkling of an Eye* (1916), p. 132.

15. *In the Twinkling of an Eye* (1916), p. 136.

16. *In the Twinkling of an Eye* (1916), p. 152.

17. *In the Twinkling of an Eye* (1916), pp. 32, 249-50.

18. *In the Twinkling of an Eye* (1916), pp. 249-50.

19. *In the Twinkling of an Eye* (1916), p. 242.

20. *The Mark of the Beast* (1915; 1974), p. 95.

21. *The Mark of the Beast* (1915; 1974), p. 103.

22. *Scarlet and Purple* (1913; 1974), p. 144; *The Mark of the Beast* (1915; 1974), p. 41.

23. *In the Twinkling of an Eye* (1916), p. 263; *Scarlet and Purple* (1913; 1974), p. 54.

24. *The Mark of the Beast* (1915; 1974), p. 110; *In the Twinkling of an Eye* (1916), p. 226.

25. *In the Twinkling of an Eye* (1916), p. 263; *Scarlet and Purple* (1913; 1974), p. 147.

26. *Scarlet and Purple* (1913; 1974), p. 160.

27. *Scarlet and Purple* (1913; 1974), p. 140; *In the Twinkling of an Eye* (1916), pp. 125-126, 177.

28. *In the Twinkling of an Eye* (1916), pp. 255, 258-9.

29. *The Mark of the Beast* (1915; 1974), pp. 30-2.

30. Joel A. Carpenter, *Revive Us Again: The Reawakening of American Fundamentalism* (Oxford: OUP, 1997), pp. 101-105.

31. *The Mark of the Beast* (1915; 1974), pp. 15-17.

32. *The Mark of the Beast* (1915; 1974), pp. 97, 58, 51.

33. *Scarlet and Purple* (1913; 1974), pp. 162-3.

34. *The Mark of the Beast* (1915; 1974), pp. 42-3, 104; *Scarlet and Purple* (1913; 1974), p. 148.

35. *The Mark of the Beast* (1915; 1974), p. 148.

36. *The Mark* (2000), pp. 84, 170.

37. *In the Twinkling of an Eye* (1916), p. 139.

38. Frederick A. Tatford, *The Clock Strikes* (London: Lakeland, 1970).

39. *The Clock Strikes* (1970), p. 7.

40. *The Clock Strikes* (1970), p. 7.

41. *The Clock Strikes* (1970), pp. 24-25.

42. This older variant of dispensationalism is endorsed in contrast to the 'progressive dispensationalism' expounded in Craig A. Blaising and Darrell L. Bock, *Progressive Dispensationalism* (Wheaton, IL: Victor, 1993).

43. *Left Behind* (1995), p. 18.

44. Mel Odom, *Apocalypse Dawn* (Wheaton, IL: Tyndale House, 2003), p. 357.

45. *Apocalypse Dawn* (2003), pp. 244-45.

46. *The Remnant* (2002), p. 343.

47. *Tribulation Force* (1996), p. 53.

48. *Tribulation Force* (1996), p. 273; J. N. D. Kelly, *The Oxford Dictionary of Popes* (Oxford: OUP, 1986), s.v.

49. *Tribulation Force* (1996), p. 279.

50. *Tribulation Force* (1996), p. 27.

51. *Tribulation Force* (1996), p. 251.

52. *Assassins* (1999), p. 50; Boyer, *When Time Shall be no More* (1992), pp. 282-83.

53. *The Mark* (2000), pp. 17, 85.

54. *The Mark* (2000), p. 156.

55. *Apollyon* (1999), pp. 104-5.

56. *Assassins* (1999), p. 354.

57. *The Mark* (2000), p. 333.

58. *Tribulation Force* (1996), pp. 150, 388, 360.

59. *Nicolae* (1997), p. 132, cf. p. 370.

60. *Apollyon* (1999), p. 61.

61. *The Mark* (2000), p. 334.

62. *Soul Harvest* (1998), p. 324.

63. *Tribulation Force* (1996), p. 29.

64. *Tribulation Force* (1996), pp. 357, 370.

65. *Tribulation Force* (1996), p. 127.

66. *Tribulation Force* (1996), p. 424; *Nicolae* (1997), p. 143.

67. *Tribulation Force* (1996), p. 444.

68. *Tribulation Force* (1996), pp. 34, 45.

69. *Tribulation Force* (1996), pp. 65-6.

70. *Nicolae* (1997), p. 359.

71. *Apollyon* (1999), p. 258.

72. *Desecration* (2001), p. 100.

73. *Apollyon* (1999), p. 295; *The Remnant* (2002), pp. 253-54; *Desecration* (2001), p. 120.

74. Tim LaHaye and Greg Dinallo, *Bablyon Rising* (London: Hodder and Stoughton, 2004), p. 9.

75. *Bablyon Rising* (2004), p. 57.

76. *Bablyon Rising* (2004), p. 44.

77. *Bablyon Rising* (2004), p. 61.

78. *Bablyon Rising* (2004), pp. 209-210.

79. *Bablyon Rising* (2004), p. 396.

80. *Bablyon Rising* (2004), pp. 248-249.

81. *Bablyon Rising* (2004), p. 354.

82. *Bablyon Rising* (2004), p. 151.

83. *Bablyon Rising* (2004), p. 172.

84. *Bablyon Rising* (2004), pp. 174, 175, 243.

85. *Bablyon Rising* (2004), pp. 7, 9.

86. Jerry B. Jenkins, *Soon: The Beginning of the End* (London: Hodder and Stoughton, 2003), p. 105.

87. This restructuring is highly ironic, in that *Assassins* (1999) was dedicated to former president of Dallas Theological Seminary, John F. Walvoord, who 'has helped keep the torch of prophecy burning'.

88. *Soul Harvest* (1998), pp. 64, 84.

89. *The Indwelling* (2000), p. 90.

90. *The Indwelling* (2000), p. 166.

91. *Assassins* (1999), p. 239.

92. *Soon* (2004), p. 35.

93. *Soon* (2004), p. 199.

94. *Soon* (2004), p. 199.

95. *Soon* (2004), p. 347.

96. *Apocalypse Dawn* (2003), p. 36.

97. *Apocalypse Dawn* (2003), p. 309.

98. *Apocalypse Dawn* (2003), pp. 305-306.

99. *Apocalypse Dawn* (2003), p. 341.

100. *Apocalypse Dawn* (2003), p. 440.

101. See also Psalm 39.

102. *Apocalypse Dawn* (2003), p. 73.

103. *Apollyon* (1999), pp. 7, 192, 357; *Assassins* (1999), p. 183; *The Mark* (2000), p. 140; *The Remnant* (2002), pp. 232, 323, 360.

104. *The Mark* (2000), p. 147.

105. *Left Behind* (1995), p. 79.

CHAPTER 4

1. *Soul Harvest* (1998), p. 134.

2. *The Mark of the Beast* (1915; 1974), p. 5

3. See http://www.jerryjenkins.com and http://www.timlahaye.com. Further details on LaHaye's career can be found in Timothy Larsen (general ed.), *Biographical Dictionary of Evangelicals* (Leicester: IVP, 2003), s.v.

4. 'Left Behind: Stronger than fiction', *Today's Christian* 40:6 (November/December 2002), p. 14.

5. http://www.wayoflife.org/fbns/leftbehind.htm

6. http://wwwmiddletownbiblechurch.org/proph/lebehind.htm, accessed 5 January 2005, contains the following review of the first *Left Behind* film: 'The most serious problem is that the GOSPEL of our Lord was LEFT BEHIND in this film (actually LEFT OUT!). There was no gospel presented anywhere in the film. The name of Christ is mentioned only 3 times in the film (during about a one minute segment, a scene where a video was being played to explain the rapture. The video was prepared by a pastor prior to the rapture with the hope that it would help people to understand what was happening after the rapture). Apart from this Christ's Name is never mentioned. When people pray to be saved it is in the most general terms ("God, please forgive me") and invitations to salvation are also very general ("You need to believe in God"). There is no mention of the cross (Christ's substitutionary death), no empty tomb, no emphasis on the sinfulness of man, no clear presentation of the terms of salvation. Any religious person who "believes in God" would probably think that they have met the conditions. I was told that Tim LaHaye had nothing to do with the making of the film and that he was troubled that the gospel was not presented. I have never read any of the books, but some

who have read the books told me they were somewhat disappointed by the movie, especially in terms of gospel content. At the end of the video one of the main actors gave an appeal to the viewers, but no gospel message was given at this point either. [Note: In the book series, there is a Catholic pope who is taken in the rapture and other Catholics as well. This is very confusing. People might wrongly think that the gospel preached by the Catholics is the same gospel found in the Bible, when they are actually diametrically opposed].'

7. *Nicolae* (1997), pp. 313-314.

8. *Left Behind* (1995), p. 90.

9. *Left Behind* (1995), p. 3.

10. *Left Behind* (1995), p. 90.

11. *Left Behind* (1995), p. 18.

12. Mel Odom, *Apocalypse Dawn* (Wheaton, IL: Tyndale House, 2003), p. 357. Neesa Hart, *End of State* (Wheaton, IL: Tyndale, 2003), p. 12.

13. *Desecration* (2001), p. 136.

14. *Nicolae* (1997), p. 314.

15. *Desecration* (2001), p. 136.

16. *The Mark* (2000), p. 358.

17. *Desecration* (2001), p. 232.

18. *The Mark* (2000), p. 319.

19. *The Remnant* (2002), p. 231.

20. *Tribulation Force* (1996), pp. 34, 45.

21. *Left Behind* (1995), p. 153.

22. *Apocalypse Dawn* (2003), p. 291.

23. *The Remnant* (2002), p. 231.

24. *The Mark* (2000), p. 319.

25. *Desecration* (2001), p. 136.

26. *The Remnant* (2002), p. 230.

27. *The Remnant* (2002), p. 230.

28. *Soul Harvest* (1998), pp. 323-324.

29. *Left Behind* (1995), p. 167.

30. *Desecration* (2001), p. 136.

31. *The Mark* (2000), p. 318.

32. *Desecration* (2001), p. 233.

33. *Apollyon* (1999), p. 190.

34. *Desecration* (2001), p. 233.

35. *Soul Harvest* (1998), pp. 132-133.

36. LaHaye and Greg Dinallo, *Bablyon Rising* (London: Hodder and Stoughton, 2004), pp. 115-116.

37. *Bablyon Rising* (2004), p. 389.

38. J. N. Darby, *Collected Writings* (Winschoten, Netherlands: H. L. Heijkoop, 1972), x. 185.

39. Darby, *Collected Writings* (1972), x. 187.

40. *Apocalypse Dawn* (2003), p. 285.

41. Note the emphasis of this theme in Amy Johnson Frykholm, *Rapture Culture:* Left Behind *in Evangelical America* (Oxford: OUP, 2004).

42. *Soul Harvest* (1998), p. 131.

43. *Left Behind* (1995), p. 74.

44. *Left Behind* (1995), p. 156.

45. *Desecration* (2001), p. 136.

46. *The Indwelling* (2000), p. 186

47. *Armageddon* (2003), p. 16.

48. *Armageddon* (2003), p. 40.

49. *Desecration* (2001), p. 103.

50. *Desecration* (2001), p. 104.

51. *The Mark* (2000), p. 183.

52. *The Mark* (2000), p. 339. The emphasis is in the original.

53. *The Remnant* (2002), p. 259.

54. *Armageddon* (2003), pp. 17-18.

55. *Apocalypse Dawn* (2003), pp. 338, 362.

56. *Apocalypse Dawn* (2003), p. 342.

57. *Apocalypse Dawn* (2003), p. 363.

58. *Apocalypse Dawn* (2003), p. 398.

CHAPTER 5

1. *Soul Harvest* (1998), p. 318.

2. *Tribulation Force* (1996), p. 236; *Desecration* (2001), p. 2.

3. *Assassins* (1999), p. 293.

4. It is interesting to note that the series also erroneously claims that the Bible calls Jerusalem 'the Eternal City'; *Armageddon*

(2003), p. 298.

5. This devotional reading is described in Amy Johnson Frykholm, *Rapture Culture: Left Behind in Evangelical America* (Oxford: OUP, 2004), p. 102.

6. Michael Williams, *This World is Not My Home: The Origins and Development of Dispensationalism* (Fearn: Mentor, 2003), p. 123.

7. See, for example, *Tribulation Force* (1996), p. 30.

8. *Assassins* (1999), p. 70.

9. *The Indwelling* (2000), p. 68.

10. *Apollyon* (1999), p. 6.

11. *The Mark* (2000), p. 265.

12. *Desecration* (2001), p. 308.

13. *The Indwelling* (2000), p. 345.

14. *Nicolae* (1997), p. 253.

15. *Desecration* (2001), pp. 288-289.

16. *Desecration* (2001), p. 363.

17. *The Indwelling* (2000), p. 77.

18. *The Indwelling* (2000), p. 71.

19. *The Indwelling* (2000), p. 76-79, 87, 232.

20. *The Indwelling* (2000), p. 232.

21. *The Indwelling* (2000), p. 70.

22. *Tribulation Force* (1996), pp. 34, 45.

23. Mel Odom, *Apocalypse Dawn* (Wheaton, IL: Tyndale House, 2003), p. 76.

24. A number of important figures in evangelical history, such as John Bunyan, have not adhered to this view.

25. *The Mark* (2000), p. 142.

26. *The Mark* (2000), p. 149.

27. *Desecration* (2001), p. 102.

CHAPTER 6

1. *Desecration* (2001), p. 179.

2. James Montgomery Boice, *The Last and Future World* (Grand Rapids, Michigan: Zondervan, 1974), p. 33.

3. Note, for example, the extreme system of preterism refuted by R. C. Sproul, *The Last Days According to Jesus: When did Jesus say he would return?* (Grand Rapids, Michigan: Baker, 1998).

4. The Rapture Index can be accessed at http://www.raptureready.com.

5. www.raptureready.com, accessed February 2005.

6. T. S. Eliot, 'The Hollow Men', in *Collected Poems, 1909-1962* (London: Faber and Faber, 1963), p. 92.

7. *Desecration* (2001), p. 179.

8. C. H. Spurgeon, *Lectures to My Students* (London: Passmore and Alabaster, 1877), p. 83.

9. John Draper, 'Anger over end times 'betrayal'', Christian Retailing Online, 6 January 2005, www.christianretailing.com/print.php?sid=323, accessed January 2005.

CHAPTER 7

1. *Armageddon* (2003), p. 392.

2. *Armageddon* (2003), p. 104.

3. *Armageddon* (2003), p. 392.

4. J. C. Ryle, *Coming Events and Present Duties* (1867), republished as *Prophecy* (Fearn, Ross-shire: Christian Focus, 1991), pp. 105, 110.

APPENDIX

1. A.A. Hoekema, *The Bible and the Future* (Grand Rapids: Eerdmans, 1979), p. 195.

2. This view is outlined in Craig A. Blaising and Darrell L. Bock, *Progressive Dispensationalism* (Wheaton, Illinois: Victor, 1993).

3. For a discussion of Carson and Piper's New Covenant theology, see www.passionforgrace.org.uk/ documents/Defining-NewCovenantTheology2.doc and www.desiringgod.org/library/theological_qa/law_gospel/disp_cov_ncov.html, both accessed December 2005.

SNC 1429